The Little Flowers of St. Francis

The Little Flowers
of
St. Francis

A Paraphrase

Donald E. Demaray

ALBA · HOUSE   NEW · YORK

SOCIETY OF ST. PAUL, 2187 VICTORY BLVD., STATEN ISLAND, NY 10314

ST PAULS

Library of Congress Cataloging-in-Publication Data

Fioretti di San Francesco. English.
    The little flowers of St. Francis: a paraphrase / [translated by] Donald Demaray.
       p. cm.
    Translation of: Fioretti di San Francesco.
    ISBN 0-8189-0618-9
    1. Francis of Assisi, Saint, 1182-1226—Legends.   I. Francis of Assisi, Saint,
    1182-1226. II. Demaray, Donald E.   III. Title.
    BX4700.F63E5 1992
    271'.302—dc20   91-42793
                                           CIP

Produced and designed in the United States of America by the
Fathers and Brothers of the Society of St. Paul,
2187 Victory Boulevard, Staten Island, New York 10314-6603
as part of their communications apostolate.

ISBN: 0-8189-0618-9

Printing Information:

Current Printing - first digit   2   3   4   5   6   7   8   9   10

Year of Current Printing - first year shown

         2000 2001 2002 2003 2004 2005 2006 2007 2008 2009

For
Kathleen
with love

She lives life to the full
in the Spirit of Christ

Acknowledgments

Warm thanks go to word processors Elizabeth Collins and David Cupps. John Seery, one of the Asbury Seminary librarians, goes beyond the call of duty. My wife, Kathleen, never fails to bring joyous encouragement in all my writing projects. Father Victor Viberti of Alba House exercises both grace and patience. Brother Aloysius Milella, Editorial Coordinator, never fails to help and encourage.

Contents

"Preach the Gospel in everything that you do;
if necessary, use words."

— *St. Francis*

Preface

The St. Francis stories speak with picture book power — power born of childlike simplicity and understanding of the world of the Spirit. No worldly sophistication has quite the same dynamic to reveal the wisdom of God. That wisdom captured Francis and saturated his very being with truth about how to live life to the full.

Brother Ugolino wrote down these accounts a century after Francis' death. (Francis died at age forty-four in 1226.) The anecdotes shine like stars on a clear night.

The picture we have of Brother Francis himself in *The Little Flowers* leads us to believe he walked in two worlds, the world called heaven more than the world on earth. He would take no money or material things for himself; if they could help someone, they served their purpose. He aided the poor, especially lepers.

Married to Lady Poverty, Francis strikes us as head over heels in love, like a young man enamored of a lovely girl. He liked nothing better than to spend whole nights in prayer. He loved Jesus Christ compassionately, lived in His world with glorious spontaneity, thought His thoughts after Him, obeyed Him with astonishing faithfulness. In this lifestyle he found freedom, and refused personal ownership of houses, lands and wealth lest they put him in prison.

Francis called others to follow Christ radically, too. In two years he had a dozen disciples; in eleven years 5,000. Happiest when his friars sacrificed everything, he never expressed more anguish than when they showed signs of greed and loss of love for Lady Poverty. His disciples must marry Poverty and never ask for divorce. No other Christian group of the time identified with total sacrifice as did the Franciscans. Francis also founded a women's order, the Poor Clares, named for the first abbess.

The St. Francis accounts first appeared in Latin, then in Italian. Many English versions have been published. The present one presents itself in newspaper English, the language of everyday talk. Christian classics like *The Little Flowers* can seem terribly distant to fast-paced moderns; I want to make the speech and spiritual truths accessible to everyone.

The easy-to-read format gives the eyes permission to run quickly along the lines. I have tried to keep to intended meanings while employing up-to-date vernacular and a somewhat paraphrastic style. And to keep the book as brief as possible, I have treated only the first forty-one chapters, which deal with St. Francis himself and his followers.

My prayer is that the gentle and generous heart of Francis, and the spiritually insightful story pictures will speak deep within readers' hearts to bring home the secrets of fulfillment.

Donald E. Demaray
Wilmore, Kentucky

The Little Flowers of St. Francis

I

The First Twelve Friends of St. Francis

First, note this:
　　St. Francis patterned his whole life
　　after Christ.
Just as Christ,
　　　　at the outset of His ministry,
　　　　selected twelve apostles
　　　　　　to reject the world,
　　　　　　to follow Him in poverty,
　　　　　　to say Yes to all virtues;
　　　　So St. Francis,
　　　　　　at the outset of his Order,
　　　　　　selected twelve friends
　　　　　　　　to follow poverty completely.
And even as one of Christ's twelve
　　　　said No to God,
　　　　and at last hanged himself;
So one of St. Francis' twelve,
　　　　Brother John of Capella,
　　　　said No to the Order,
　　　　and at last hanged himself
　　　　　　with a rope.
　　　　　　　　To the elect this is
　　　　　　　　　　a great lesson,
　　　　　　　　　　a reason for humility,
　　　　　　　　　　a reason for fear,
　　　　　　　　　　　　since no one
　　　　　　　　　　　　can merely assume
　　　　　　　　　　　　he will persevere
　　　　　　　　　　　　to the end
　　　　　　　　　　　　in God's grace.

And even as the Apostles were,
    for the whole world to see,
        wonders of goodness and
        filled with God's Spirit,
So St. Francis' friends were,
    for the whole world to see,
        the most wonderful men,
        the most holy,
            since the Apostles.
    Brother Giles
        was caught up to the third heaven
            like St. Paul.
    Brother Philip — he was tall —
        was touched on the lips
            by an angel
            with a burning coal
                like Isaiah.
    Brother Silvester — virginally pure —
        was on speaking terms
        with God
            like Moses.
    Brother Bernard — very humble —
        with his keen mind,
            saw life in the light of Wisdom
            (like the eagle, John the Evangelist),
        and explained Scripture profoundly.
    Brother Ruffino — a nobleman of Assisi —
        sanctified by God,
        made a saint by heaven,
            while still living and
            as though sanctified in his mother's womb,
                proved himself strongly
                loyal to Christ.
So all Francis' friends
    carried the marks of
    godliness.

II

Brother Bernard's Conversion

St. Francis' first companion,
Brother Bernard of Assisi,
came to conversion
like this:
St. Francis was
still in everyday clothes,
yet looking contemptible
and doing penance.
People called him simple-minded
— they laughed,
insulted,
threw stones,
flung mud —
both relatives and strangers.
St. Francis nonetheless
experienced God's sustaining power,
knew the Spirit's peace,
and thus took
insults and scorn
with joy on his face
and as if deaf and dumb.
Well now, Lord Bernard,
one of the richest,
one of the wisest
noblemen of all Assisi,
whose decisions everyone respected
— this Lord did a lot of thinking.
He thought about
how Francis turned his back totally on the world,
how Francis exhibited such patience under insult,

3

how Francis handled two years of scorn
— he always appeared peaceful and even-tempered.
These thoughts made Bernard say inwardly,
"Clearly, this Francis fellow
has something!"
It's no surprise, then, that
Bernard invited St. Francis
to dinner one evening.
The saint humbly accepted.
But Bernard really wanted
to put St. Francis to the test.
So he invited Francis to stay all night.
Francis humbly agreed.
Bernard made up a bed in his own room
and kept a light burning.
Francis went right to bed.
Bernard, planning to watch all night,
went to bed
pretending to sleep,
even snoring loudly.
Francis, thinking Bernard asleep,
got out of bed and
fell to his knees in fervent prayer:
"My God! My All!"
he cried in tears.
This simple devotion he repeated
until time for morning worship
in the church.
St. Francis prayed this
while meditating
on the Almighty God's goodness
and compassion
for a needy world
(God would use Francis
to help the world).
Francis, by the Spirit of prophecy,
saw what God would do
with his Order,

but also how little Francis could do
without grace.
Thus his prayer,
"My God! My All!"
Well! Bernard witnessed all this
in the light of the burning lamp,
and while looking and pondering,
the Holy Spirit touched him in his depths
and motivated him to change his life.
So, when the sun came up
he had a word with St. Francis:
"Brother Francis, I've made a clear decision
to leave the world
and do whatever you assign."
At this, St. Francis replied with much joy,
"Because what you say is so great and profound,
we will consult our Lord Jesus Christ,
so He Himself can show us His will
and teach us how to do it.
Come, let's go to church to see the priest,
and ask him to say a Mass;
After that we will wait until 9 a.m. prayers.
In our praying, we will humbly ask for
three messages from the missal."
All this pleased Bernard.
So they went to the church.
After Mass and prayers
the priest took the missal;
he made the sign of the cross,
then opened the missal three times
in the name of our Lord Jesus Christ.
The message from the first opening —
The words of Christ to the young man:
"To be perfect
Sell everything you have,
Give the proceeds to the poor,
Follow Me."
The message from the second opening —

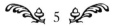

The words of Christ when He sent the Apostles to preach:
  "Take nothing with you;
    No staff,
    No travel case,
    No food,
    No money."
  In this, Jesus wanted to teach them
    To rely totally on God,
    To give complete attention to preaching
      the Good News.
The message from the third opening —
  The words of Christ:
    "If you wish to come to Me,
    Deny yourself,
    Take up your cross,
    Follow Me."
So when they got these three messages,
  St. Francis said to Bernard,
    "We now know Christ's counsel.
    Go and do exactly what He says.
    Blessed be our Lord Jesus Christ
      for so graciously
      showing us His Gospel way of life!"
At once the wealthy Bernard
  produced all he owned and
  sold every bit of it.
    With great joy
    he gave all the money
    to the poor.
      Carrying the money in his shirt,
      he gave lots away
      in a spirit of generosity
        to widows,
        orphans,
        pilgrims,
        monasteries
        and hospitals.
  St. Francis stood by Bernard

in all this
and helped him.
A man named Silvester,
   watching Francis,
      suffered an attack of greed:
         "You owe me more
         for the stones you bought
         to repair churches."
Francis refused to argue,
but marveling at his greed,
followed the Gospel
in giving to any and all who asked.
     He filled Silvester's shirt
     with money
     from Bernard's shirt;
     Then said,
         "If you ask more,
         I will give you more."
     But Silvester was happy now
         and went home.
Later that evening,
Silvester had long thoughts,
     grew sorry about his greed,
       meditated on Bernard's devotion to Christ
       and on Francis' holy life.
On three successive nights
God gave Silvester this vision:
     A gold cross
     coming out of Francis' mouth;
     The top of the cross going up to heaven;
     The arms east and west to the end of the world.
Through this vision
     God touched Silvester;
     he sold his property
     and gave the proceeds
        to the poor.
     Later he joined St. Francis' Order,
       and became so holy he spoke with God

as a friend,
like St. Francis did several times.
Likewise, Bernard,
after giving everything away for God,
received a great deal of grace,
so much so that
Christ absorbed him in
unbroken contemplation
from time to time.
Francis told people to honor Bernard,
that he had really founded the Order
because he was the first to live
Gospel poverty
by distributing to the poor,
and by keeping nothing for himself,
but giving himself totally to Christ
The Crucified.
We must always bless the memory of
Bernard.
Yes, by all means.
May Christ be blessed forever. Amen.

III

The Humility and Obedience of St. Francis and Brother Bernard

Francis,
    nearly blind from penance and continuous weeping,
    could hardly even see light.
    One day he went to
        Brother Bernard
        to talk about God.
        He found Bernard
        in the woods
        absorbed in God,
        at one with Him.
            "Come, speak with this blind man,"
            Francis called.
        But Bernard was lost in God.
Brother Bernard neither answered St. Francis
        nor went to him;
        Bernard, a great contemplative,
                his consciousness suspended,
                was in God's presence.
Brother Bernard, St. Francis knew from experience,
            had a special gift
            to talk about God.
            That's why St. Francis
            wanted to visit with Bernard.
So again Francis called;
        in fact, he called twice:
            "Come, speak with this blind man."
        But Brother Bernard did not hear,
                    answer, or go to him.
So Francis went away,

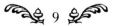

a little disappointed,
and a little complaining:
   "Didn't he want to respond?"
   St. Francis had these thoughts
      walking along a path,
      and he said to his walking companion:
        "Wait here a minute."
        Francis went to a quiet spot
        to pray,
           begging God to say
           why Brother Bernard
           didn't answer him.
        God said to him in prayer,
          "Why trouble yourself,
          you poor little fellow?
          Can you expect someone
          to leave God
          for any creature?
          Brother Bernard, absorbed in Me,
          could not leave Me.
          Therefore don't act surprised;
          so unconscious of surroundings
          was Bernard,
          that he couldn't even hear you."
  At this answer from God,
Francis went very fast to Brother Bernard,
    in humility to accuse himself
    of thoughts against Bernard.
But the saintly Bernard saw Francis coming,
    and threw himself at Francis' feet.
      And with that,
        the humility of Francis
        and the love and reverence of Bernard
          came together.
  St. Francis made Bernard get up,
    then told him
      his thoughts,
      his anxiety,

his message — God's reprimand.
Francis closed the conversation —
"In holy obedience,
do whatever I command."
Brother Bernard feared Francis
would order something excessive,
as he often did.
(He wanted to avoid
anything like that.)
So Bernard said,
"I'll do what you command
if you do what I command."
Then Brother Bernard asked for
Francis' command.
Francis ordered:
"Punish my presumption and insolence
this way:
I'll lie on my back;
You put one foot on my throat
and one foot on my mouth,
stepping on me this way
three times
side to side.
And while you do that say,
'Stay on your back,
you country clodhopper,
son of Peter Bernardone.'
Insult me more —
'How can you be so proud,
you worthless creature?'"
Brother Bernard heard this,
but found it hard to obey.
Yet, holy obedience made him do it,
for St. Francis had commanded it.
Brother Bernard did his duty
as courteously as possible.
When done, Francis said,
"Now Brother Bernard,

command whatever you wish,
for I promised to obey you."
So Brother Bernard responded this way:
"In holy obedience
do this when we're together:
Scold and correct me harshly
for my faults."
Well! Francis heard this with surprise
for Brother Bernard was very holy
— Francis respected him greatly —
and saw no reason to correct him.
No wonder, then, that
St. Francis avoided staying very long
with him
in order to avoid correcting
this very saintly brother.
Yet he hungered
to see Brother Bernard,
to hear him talk about God.
Wonderful were St. Francis' conflicts
and Brother Bernard's too!
Obedience and charity,
Patience and humility
came into conflict.
Wonderful, too, and inspirational
was St. Francis'
love,
reverence,
and humility
in his treatment of,
in his speech about
Brother Bernard.
This story of St. Francis and Brother Bernard
leads us to praise and glorify Christ.

IV

St. Francis and St. James' Church;
Brother Elias and the Angel

At the beginning of St. Francis' Order,
  before he had very many friars,
  before they had regular meeting places,
    St. Francis went
        to St. James' Church in Galicia*
        to pray;
            He took some friends,
            including Brother Bernard.
  On the way and along the road,
      they found a poor sick man;
      St. Francis took pity on him
      and said to Brother Bernard:
          "My son,
          stay here
          and care for this poor man."
  Brother Bernard quickly and humbly,
      communicating reverence and respect
      by bending his knee and bowing his head,
          accepted Francis' assignment.
          So he stayed right there
              while St. Francis and his friends
              went on to St. James' Church.
St. Francis spent the night
  in prayer
  in St. James' Church,
      And God gave him a revelation:
          He must plant houses all over the world,

---

* This is the famous Shrine of St. James at Compostella, to which many pilgrims still
  travel. Galicia is a region in Spain.

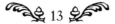

because the Order would fan out
and include a lot of friars.
'This revelation marked the beginning
of Francis' work
founding friaries in many areas.
St. Francis now retraced his steps
along the road to the shrine.
There he met Brother Bernard
and the sick man
now completely recovered.
At this, St. Francis told Brother Bernard
he could go to St. James'.
In the meantime,
St. Francis returned
to the Valley of Spoleto.
In that friary,
St. Francis stayed with
Brother Masseo and Brother Elias
and some others.
They all respected Francis
and his times of prayer;
They knew God spoke great things
to Francis in prayer.
One day while St. Francis prayed,
a handsome lad
knocked in a spirit of dire necessity,
and without stopping.
"What on earth could this mean?"
the brothers wondered.
Brother Masseo answered the door:
"Well! whatever's on your mind?
Have you never knocked on a friar's door?"
"How am I supposed to knock?"
Brother Masseo said that he should
knock three times,
then pause
to allow time for a brother to say
The Lord's Prayer;
If no answer by then,

knock once more.
"But," said the young man,
   "I'm in a terrible hurry;
   You see, I've come a long distance
   — that explains my boisterous knocking —
   And I want to see Brother Francis.
   But he's lost in contemplation
   in the forest,
      and I'd better not disturb him
      So may I see Brother Elias?
      He's wise, I'm told,
      and I need to ask about something."
Brother Masseo went to tell Brother Elias
   to see the young man;
   But, proud and testy,
   Brother Elias got angry,
   and refused to go.
      At this, Brother Masseo found himself
      between a rock and a hard place:
         "If I say Brother Elias can't come,
            I'll be lying;
         If I say Brother Elias is angry,
            that Brother Elias will not come,
            then I'll be giving scandal."
In the meantime,
   while Brother Masseo delayed,
   the young man knocked like he did before.
   So the friar returned to the gate,
   and said to the young man,
      "You didn't knock as I told you."
Well! that young man,
God's angel,
   detected the truth:
      "Brother Elias doesn't want to come;
      go tell Brother Francis
         I've come to see him,
         but I don't want to disturb him
         so he must tell Elias to come."
So Brother Masseo saw Brother Francis

praying with his face towards heaven;
He told him about the young man
and also about Brother Elias.
Without moving,
   Brother Francis said,
     "Tell Brother Elias
      to go to the young man immediately,
      and that under obedience."
Well! When Brother Elias heard that,
   he went in such anger
   that he opened the gate tempestuously,
   really disturbing the peace,
   saying to the young man,
     "What do *you* want?"
The young fellow replied,
   "I want to know
     if it's alright for Gospel followers
     to eat anything offered,
     as Christ indicated to His disciples.
   "I also want to know
     if it's alright for someone to insist
     that followers of the Gospel
     do something against Christian liberty."
Brother Elias, full of pride,
   said he knew the answer
   but would not tell it;
   "Go on your way," he cried.
The youth declared,
   "I have better knowledge
   of the answer than you do!"
At that Brother Elias heaved the gate shut
   and walked away.
   But as he started to think about the question
   he puzzled over it;
   he couldn't put his finger on the answer.
     Brother Elias' problem?
      When Vicar of his Order,
      he made a bold rule
      beyond the Gospel,

beyond St. Francis' rule:
No friar could eat meat.
Well! Brother Elias had a problem.
He saw *himself* the target
of the young man's question.
He did not know how to solve his problem.
More, the humble youth declared
he could answer the question
better than Brother Elias.
So Brother Elias went to the gate again,
intending to ask the question
of the young man.
Alas! the man had gone.
Even by searching everywhere
Elias could not find him.
The angel wouldn't wait
because pride does not deserve
to talk with angels.
This incident over,
St. Francis knowing it all by revelation
came out of the woods
to give Brother Elias
a real dressing down.
Speaking forcefully, St. Francis said,
"Do you know why your proud behavior is wrong?
You drive away angels
sent to visit and instruct us.
Listen!
I have this terrible fear
that your arrogance
will push you out of our Order,
that you will finish your days
away from us."
The prophecy came true.
Elias died outside the Order.
On the very day,
at the very hour
the angel disappeared,
he appeared to Brother Bernard

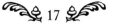

returning from St. James'.
Brother Bernard came to a river
he could not cross,
he stood on the bank of the wide river.
  The angel spoke to Brother Bernard
  in Bernard's native tongue:
    "God's peace to you, good brother."
Brother Bernard,
    really impressed,
    marveled at the young man's
      good looks,
      use of language,
      peaceful "Hello,"
      happy manner.
  Brother Bernard asked,
    "Where do you come from,
    fine young man?"
  The angel answered:
    "Where St. Francis was.
    I went there to talk with him,
    but couldn't
    because he had lost himself
    talking with God in the woods;
    I didn't wish to disturb him.
    Brothers Giles, Elias and Masseo
    stayed near St. Francis.
    Brother Masseo instructed me
    in gate-knocking — the friars' way.
    But Brother Elias,
    not wanting to answer my question,
    later suffered regret,
      and wished to hear and see me,
      but couldn't."
  Having said that,
  the angel asked Brother Bernard:
    "Dear friend,
  why do you hesitate
  to cross the river?"
"Because," said Brother Bernard,

"I look into the deep water
and grow fearful."
    So the angel said,
        "Let's cross together;
        then you won't panic."
The angel took his hand,
and at once put Brother Bernard
on the other side of the river.
    Then Brother Bernard knew
    that the man was
    God's angel!
    With immense devotion,
    with reverence,
    with joy,
        Brother Bernard said loudly,
            "You wonderful angel,
            tell me your name."
    The angel asked,
        "Why do you want to know my name,
        wonderful as it is?"
With that,
    the angel disappeared,
    leaving the Brother
    happy and joyful
    for the remainder of his trip.
Brother Bernard made a note of
    the day,
    the hour,
        the angel came to him.
When he came to St. Francis and the others,
Brother Bernard told the whole story,
even to details.
That's why they knew for certain
        that the same angel
        came to both places,
    the same day,
    the same hour.
        And they expressed gratitude
        to God. Amen.

V

Brother Bernard Goes to Bologna

God called St. Francis and his friends
to bear Christ's cross
    in their hearts,
    in their acts,
    in their language.
        They experienced crucifixion
            in their deeds,
            in their disciplined living.
        They liked this and wanted
            more dishonor,
            more affronts,
                because they loved Christ.
        They liked this much better than
            worldly reputation,
            worldly honors,
            human esteem.
        They did, in fact, rejoice
            in mistreatment.
        They became sad
            by being honored.
        They walked about
            like pilgrims and strangers,
                just taking Christ crucified
                with them.
        They proved themselves
            real branches of the
            real vine, Christ.
        They produced
            good fruit
                — souls won for God.

In the early days of St. Francis' Order,
he sent Brother Bernard to Bologna
    so he could,
    by God's grace given him,
    produce good fruit
    for the Lord.
        So Brother Bernard,
        with the power of the cross,
        went in holy obedience to Bologna.
There in Bologna,
children seeing him dressed crudely,
made fun of him by
    mockery,
    insult,
    hitting.
        Children do these things to simpletons.
Brother Bernard showed patience and joy
    in all this
    because he loved Christ.
He wanted more mockery,
    so he went to the town's square
    where children and grown-ups
        gathered about him.
        Some pulled his hood,
        some threw dust,
        some threw stones,
        some pushed him
            now one way,
            now the other.
Brother Bernard kept calm,
    he stayed patient,
    he remained happy,
    he refused to complain,
    he would not go away;
        in fact,
        he went to the square
        many days
        so he could endure

more hurt.
Well! perfection issues from patience;
And patience proves goodness.
So a lawyer,
thinking about Brother Bernard's
consistency and goodness
— Bernard never got disturbed
not even by injury,
not even by insult
after many days —
said to himself,
"That man's got to be a saint!"
He went right to Brother Bernard
to ask,
"Who in the world are you?
Why are you here?"
Brother Bernard answered by
reaching in his robe
and taking out the Rule of St. Francis,
then giving it to the lawyer to read.
When the lawyer read it all,
he reflected on its high level of perfection,
stood amazed,
and with admiration said to his friends,
"I have never seen such a
high form of religious life!
This man and his friends
have to be some of the
saintliest men in the world.
So anybody who insults him
commits a terrible sin;
Brother Bernard deserves honors,
not insults.
Really, he is God's genuine friend."
Then he spoke to Brother Bernard:
"If I can provide a place
for you to serve,
I will do it for my own soul's good."

Brother Bernard replied,
    "I believe your offer is inspired
    by God,
    so I happily accept it
    to honor Christ."
Then the lawyer took Brother Bernard,
    with a lot of joy and love,
    to his home,
    and later gave him the promised
    place from which to serve.
        The lawyer paid for it
        out of his own pocket.
    From that time,
    the lawyer cared for
        Brother Bernard and his friends.
Now Brother Bernard got to be
greatly honored by those who knew
about him
    because of the purity
        of his talk.
People even wanted to touch him,
        to see him,
        to hear him,
            so they could be blessed
            by him.
But this bothered Brother Bernard:
    Genuine and modest followers of Christ
    get afraid of the world's honor;
        that, you know, can clog the channels
        of peace and wholeness.
    So he left that place
    to return to St. Francis.
        To St. Francis he said:
            "We've now established a
            friary in Bologna.
            Send friars there
                to live and
                to keep it going.

I'm no longer getting
the job done there;
    In fact, because of
    grandiose honor to me,
    I might lose more than
    I gain."
Well, Francis,
learning in detail
how the Lord had used Brother Bernard,
    praised God
    who had started to spread
    the poor little disciples of the Cross
    for the people's salvation.
    Later on, Francis
    sent other co-workers
        to Bologna and
        to Lombardy,
        and there they established
        many friaries.
No wonder we praise Jesus,
no wonder we show respect to Jesus.
Amen.

VI

St. Francis' Love of Brother Bernard; St. Francis' Death and Brother Bernard's Death

Brother Bernard was so saintly that
St. Francis honored him with total respect;
    frequently Francis said beautiful
    things about him.
One day as St. Francis prayed,
the Lord revealed to him that
    Brother Bernard,
    in the providence of God,
    would suffer vicious attacks
    by demons.
        That's why St. Francis,
        for many days,
        prayed compassionately and with tears
        for Brother Bernard,
        whom he loved like his own son.
        Francis gave him to the Lord
        Jesus Christ,
        so He in turn would give him victory
        over every testing.
            One day while Francis prayed
            with fervor,
            the Lord gave an answer:
                "Don't be afraid, Francis,
                because every testing
                comes with God's permission
                and for this reason:
                        to bring out the steel in him and
                        to put an eternal crown on his head.
                        He will win over all enemies!"

Well! Francis became ecstatic
and gave very devout thanks to the Lord
Jesus Christ.
From that moment on,
he never had an anxious thought
about Brother Bernard,
  but loved him more and more
  and with mounting joy;
  now Francis treated him with
  even greater respect.
Francis showed that love to Brother Bernard,
not only during his lifetime,
but in death as well.
  Francis lay dying,
  his devout sons around him,
  as Jacob's sons were when he died,
  weeping and grieving.
    Francis asked,
    "My first-born son —
    Where is he? He must come
    so I can bless him
    before I die."
But Brother Bernard whispered to
Brother Elias, head of the Order,
    "Slip to the saint's right hand
    so he can bless *you*."
Brother Elias went to the saint's right side,
    but when Francis put his hand on his head,
    he knew,
    even though he could not see because
    his much weeping had blinded him,
    the man was not Brother Bernard.
      "This head does not belong to
      Brother Bernard,
      my first-born."
Then Brother Bernard went to Francis' left hand,
    and St. Francis crossed his arms,
    putting his left hand on Brother Elias,

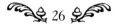

and his right hand on Brother Bernard,
and said to him:
"May God, Father of our Lord Jesus Christ,
bless you with every heavenly blessing.
You are the first-born,
God's chosen one
to show the pattern of Gospel living,
to follow poverty.
You gave away all your possessions;
you gave it all to the poor
because you loved Christ.
You did more:
You presented yourself to God
in the beauty of gentle sacrifice
to serve this Order.
That's why I want to give you a blessing,
the blessing of our Lord Jesus Christ,
and my blessing, too,
though I am a poor servant.
I want you to be blessed
with everlasting blessings while you
walk,
stand,
live and breathe,
sleep,
work,
die.
All who bless you shall be blessed;
all who curse you
will be punished in return.
You are the leader of the Order;
the friars will obey you.
Take authority to govern admissions,
also to expel.
None of the brothers have authority
over you;
you must take initiative
to follow your inclinations."

Well, after Francis' death,
the brothers loved and respected
Brother Bernard,
looking to him as their revered father.
    So when Brother Bernard came to
    his own death,
    lots of brothers came
    from here and there in the world.
        One was that heavenly spirit,
        Brother Giles;
        When he saw Brother Bernard,
        he cried out with enormous joy,
            "Lift up your heart, Brother Bernard!
            Lift up your heart!"
        Brother Bernard whispered to someone,
        "Go prepare a place where Brother Giles
        can meditate."
        It was done.
Brother Bernard came to his last hour.
He requested, "Prop me up."
Then he said,
    "You very dear brothers,
    I don't need to say very much,
    but I do need to remind you that,
        I once stood where you now stand;
        Someday you will lie where I lie.
        Quite honestly,
        I would have given up
        a thousand worlds
        for this life of Christ-filled service.
            But I blame only myself
            for my faults;
            I confess that to my Lord and Savior,
            Jesus Christ,
            and to you, too.
        I plead with you, my very dear brothers,
        to love each other."
    After these words,

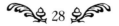

28

and some more words of wisdom,
he lay back down,
    and his face glowed with joy,
    so much so that the brothers stood
    astonished!
    In all that radiance,
    Brother Bernard passed from
    earth to heaven
    to live the fulfilled life
    of the angels.
We praise Christ,
we glorify Christ,
Amen.

VII

St. Francis' Fast Through Lent

St. Francis,
truly Christ's servant,
truly like Christ,
was given to the world to save people.
His gift to do things like Christ is
    shown
              in Francis' group of twelve,
              in the Stigmata,*
              in the forty days' fast.
On Carnival Day,
St. Francis went to the Lake of Perugia
    to visit a dear disciple and
    to sleep the night.
        There God gave him an idea:
           Spend Lent on an island in the lake.
    Francis asked his friend
    to show love to Christ
    by ferrying him to the island.
        The small boat took Francis
        to the unoccupied island
        during Ash Wednesday night
        and no one knew about it.
           Francis took only two small loaves.
           Francis asked his friend to
               tell no one about his
              island stay,
              and not to return before Holy Thursday.

---

* The Stigmata are the wounds of Christ, given St. Francis in his body, on
  September 14, 1224 during his retreat on Mt. La Verna.

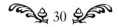

The friend went back to his home;
St. Francis stayed alone.
    Francis found no building to live in,
    so he entered a heavy thicket:
        The thorns and brush made him a residence.
        There he prayed and thought about
        heavenly matters.
        There he also remained for forty days,
        not eating,
        nor drinking,
            except for eating half a loaf.
On Holy Thursday his friend came for Francis.
    He noticed the two loaves,
    half of one eaten.
        Some believe Francis ate the half
        to keep him from pride and
        to distinguish his fast
        from Christ's forty days
        (Christ ate nothing).
            Thus Francis wanted to avoid vainglory,
            yet somehow to imitate
            Christ's forty day fast.
Later in that place where Francis fasted,
God honored the saint
by doing miracles on the island.
    People built houses there,
            lived there,
            even constructed a castle there.
    A large village grew up,
    also a house for friars,
        "The Friary of the Island."
To this day people express profound appreciation
for the place where St. Francis fasted.

VIII

St. Francis Teaches Brother Leo About Real Joy

On a winter's day
St. Francis and Brother Leo,
    walking from Perugia to St. Mary of the Angels,
    shivered and shook from the cold.
        St. Francis talked as they walked:
            "Brother Leo, I pray God
            will make the friars in our Order
            examples of holy and constructive living
            in every part of the world.
            But you must know in your heart
            that real joy
            cannot come in this."
        After walking a bit further,
        Francis talked some more:
            "Brother Leo, even if a friar
            makes the blind see,
            heals paralytics,
            drives demons away,
            brings hearing to the deaf,
            makes cripples walk,
            causes the dumb to speak,
            resurrects the dead after four days in the grave
            — none of these acts brings joy."
    A little later, in a forceful voice,
    Francis spoke again:
            "Brother Leo, if a friar
            speaks all languages,
            possesses all knowledge,
            knows all Scripture,
                 can predict the whole future and

reveal the secrets of hearts
— this won't bring joy either."
Further down the road,
Francis spoke loudly again:
"Brother Leo, God's little lamb,
Although a friar
talks like an angel,
proves himself a fine astronomer,
becomes a knowledgeable herbalist,
knows all of earth's treasures,
Knows
birds,
fish,
men,
animals,
plants,
rocks,
water
— Well, all that accumulated expertise
won't yield true joy."
Once more and a little further on,
Francis cried out,
"Brother Leo, even if a friar is
an evangelist so good he
converts all infidels to faith
— that won't produce joy either."
Well! St. Francis talked like this
for two miles.
Brother Leo asked in amazed wonder,
"Where, then, in God's Name,
do I discover real joy?"
St. Francis replied,
"When we arrive at St. Mary of the Angels
soaked through with rain,
frozen with cold,
splattered with mud,
ill with hunger,
rejected angrily at the door,

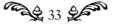

the gate keeper asking,
    'Who are you?'
We answer,
    'Two of your friars.'
He replies,
    'Nonsense! In fact,
    you are evil men,
    lying to the world and
    taking money from the poor.'
The gate keeper refuses to let us in,
so we stay in the snow and rain,
chilled and famished,
right through the night;
When we put up with all these abuses,
        all this cruelty,
        all these rejections
        without getting angry,
        without talking back to the gate keeper,
        and with humility,
            with love,
            with trust in the gate keeper and in God;
            Oh! Brother Leo,
                that is real joy!
More! If we knock on and on and
the gate keeper comes to us thoroughly indignant,
accusing us of persistent loitering;
if he uses strong language,
hits us with his fists,
then commands,
    'Get out of here
    you miserable thieves;
    Go to the shelter for beggars;
    you cannot eat or sleep in this place!'
        If we put up with all this
        patiently and peacefully,
        Oh! Brother Leo,
            this is real joy!
Further, if hunger,

cold and
the night
force us to keep on knocking,
even with tears and pleading,
    for God's sake to let us in;
    and the gate keeper becomes more angry
    and cries,
        'These miserable shameless loiterers
        force me to deal brutally';
        and he descends on us with
            a gnarled club,
        and he grabs our clothing,
        and throws us into the dirt,
        and kicks and rolls us
        over and over in the snow,
        and hits us with the club —
            yet, for Christ's love
            we behave with patience and cheer,
            focusing on Jesus' sufferings;
                Oh! Brother Leo,
                this is real joy!
So, Brother Leo, the conclusion is this:
    The Spirit's best gift,
    His highest grace,
        Christ gives to His friends:
        To conquer self
        for Jesus' sake;
            this makes us willing to go through
                sufferings,
                hurts,
                rejections,
                troubles of all sorts.
    We cannot glory in other gifts
    because they come from God,
    not us.
        So why compliment yourself
        for what God does?
    But we can glory

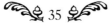

35

in troubles and sufferings
— they are ours.
That's why St. Paul says,
'I glory only
in the cross of the Lord
Jesus Christ.'
To Him belongs respect,
also reverence,
until the world's end. Amen."

IX

St. Francis and Brother Leo at Morning Prayers

During the early days of the Order,
on one occasion when St. Francis
had no book for morning prayers,
    he said to Brother Leo,
        "Dear Friend,
        we have no prayer book
        this morning,
        so we will praise God
        as I tell you.
            I will talk like this:
                'Oh! Brother Francis,
                you deserve hell
                because of all your sins.'
            Then, Brother Leo, you will say,
                'Francis, you tell the truth;
                you deserve hell.'"
Brother Leo,
with the simplicity of a dove,
agreed to this gladly:
    "Begin in God's Name."
So St. Francis declared,
    "Oh! Brother Francis,
    you've sinned so much in this world
    that you deserve hell in the next world."
Brother Leo replied,
    "God uses you to do so much good
    that you will go to heaven."
But Francis said,
    "Don't say that!

When I say I've sinned so badly
I must go to hell,
You say, 'True!
 You must live with the damned.'"
Brother Leo replied,
 "Yes, of course, gladly."
Then Francis sighed,
  wept,
  hit his breast,
  and bemoaned,
    "God of heaven and earth,
    I've sinned so often;
    I've done evil against you so much,
    that I'm totally damned."
Brother Leo responded,
 "God aims to make you so special
 you will know enormous joy."
St. Francis stood amazed.
Brother Leo answered exactly opposite
of the way Francis instructed him.
So he scolded Brother Leo:
 "Why won't you say
 what I tell you?
 In holy obedience
 I command you
 to say what I instruct.
 So I will say,
  'Oh! Little Francis,
  you're wretched
  so don't expect God to have mercy
  even though He is Mercy,
  even though He is Comfort.
  You just aren't worthy of forgiveness.'
Brother Leo, Little Lamb,
answer,
  'Right! You can't possibly
  find mercy because
  you aren't worthy.' "

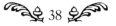

But when St. Francis announced,
    "You very bad man,
    Brother Francis," etc.,
        Brother Leo returned,
          "God the Father's forgiveness,
          incalculably bigger than your sins,
          will indeed give you mercy,
          and add a whole lot of other graces too."
Thinking about Brother Leo's answer,
showing anger yet sweetness,
showing irritation yet patience,
he said to Brother Leo,
    "Such presumption!
    You won't obey me;
    You answer every time
        just the opposite of my instructions."
Brother Leo, humbly respectful, said,
    "God being my witness,
    I fully intended to talk as you directed;
    but God tells me to say something else."
So an amazed Francis said,
    "I plead with you,
    in all love,
    answer now as I direct you."
Brother Leo thought that at last
he could follow instructions.
St. Francis said with tears,
    "Oh! Little Francis,
    very bad brother,
    do you assume God's mercy?"
Brother Leo responded:
    "You're going to receive
    unbelievable graces;
    you're going to be honored
    for all eternity.
    Why?
        Those who humble themselves
        receive honor.

I cannot say anything but
this good word,
for God talks through me."
Well, with that humble argumentation,
with lots of tears,
with enormous spiritual comfort,
the two men prayed
through the night until dawn.
Praise to Christ. Amen.

X

Brother Masseo and St. Francis: True Humility

St. Francis
lived at the Portiuncula with Brother Masseo,
whom he loved because of his
    extraordinary saintliness,
    remarkable discretion and grace
        in talking about God.
Francis came from the woods one day,
where he had cloistered himself in prayer.
    Brother Masseo tested Francis' humility:
        "Why you?
        Why you?
        Why you?"
    Francis answered,
        "What are you getting at?"
    Brother Masseo answered,
        "Why do you have so many followers?
        Why do people want to see you?
        Why do they want to hear you?
        Why do they want to obey you?
        You're not good looking.
        You're not sophisticated.
        You have no blue blood in your veins.
        Why, then, do people want *you*?"
St. Francis' heart now sang with joy;
he lifted his face to heaven,
    his soul lost in God for the longest time.
    Coming back to earth,
    Francis knelt,
        thanked God,
        spoke to Brother Masseo energetically:

"Why does this happen to me?
Why me?
Why so many followers?
The answer comes from Divine Eyes
    which see into good and evil.
    Those Divine Eyes see me as
    the worst of sinners,
    the most wretched,
    the most inadequate.
To do His wonderful work,
He finds
    no viler person anywhere;
So He chooses me to puzzle
    the noble,
    the proud,
    the strong,
    the worldly models,
    the sophisticated.
Why?
To reveal that
    every virtue,
    every good,
    comes from God,
    not from people;
To reveal that
    no one can be stuck up;
    all must depend on God,
    who alone deserves eternal credit."
Well! Brother Masseo,
    hearing these humble answers
    spoken so strongly,
        stood awestruck.
        "Francis is rooted in
        genuine humility,"
            he said to himself.
Praise to Christ. Amen.

XI

Out of Foolishness, Wisdom

One day St. Francis and Brother Masseo
walked along a road,
Brother Masseo a bit ahead.
　　They came to three roads,
　　　　One to Siena,
　　　　One to Florence,
　　　　One to Arezzo.
　　　　　　"Which shall we take?"
　　　　　　asked Brother Masseo.
St. Francis said they would go
where God willed.
　　　　"And how can we know God's will?"
　　　　asked Brother Masseo.
St. Francis answered:
　　　　"I'll show you;
　　　　do what I say in holy obedience.
　　　　Whirl around and around like a child;
　　　　don't stop until I tell you."
Brother Masseo went around and around,
then fell down from dizziness.
He did this over and again.
Finally St. Francis said,
　　　　"Stop!"
He spoke again:
　　　　"Brother Masseo, toward which city
　　　　do you look now?"
Brother Masseo replied,
　　　　"Toward Siena."
Whereupon Francis announced,
　　　　"Then that's where God wants us to go."

On the way to Siena,
Brother Masseo marveled very much
    about what Francis made him do,
    about the child-like whirling,
    about the people who watched him spin around.
Yet, respect for Francis closed his mouth.
As the two came close to Siena,
    the townspeople, having heard St. Francis would come,
    showed their respect by carrying him
    and Brother Masseo
                to the bishop's house.
While all this went on,
    some citizens of Siena fought each other,
    two actually dying.
Francis arrived,
    preached with devotion and such saintliness
    that peace came,
    issuing in friendship and harmony among the fighters!
        The bishop of Siena heard all this,
        invited Francis home,
        honored him,
        kept him all day
        and through the night.
            In the early morning,
            the humble Francis left
            with Brother Masseo
            without saying a thing!
                But Brother Masseo said to himself:
                    "This Francis!
                    He makes me spin;
                    He leaves without a thank you;
                    He seems thoughtless."
                Then God spoke:
                    "Brother Masseo,
                    Pride cannot judge divine works;
                    Pride calls for big trouble.
                    Yesterday Francis performed miracles
                      like an angel.

If he commands you to throw stones,
 do it!
I work through Francis —
  Observe the good results!
  Had fighting continued,
  more would have died,
  and the devil would have sent
   more to hell.
So don't allow pride,
  don't permit foolish thinking
   against God's obvious working!"
Well! All Masseo's inner dialogue
God revealed to Francis
as the two men walked.
  So Francis said,
   "Get a firm hold on your
   godly thoughts;
   they come from inspiration.
    Your negative thoughts reflect
     blindness,
     vanity,
     pride.
      Devils put bad thoughts
      in our minds."
Now Brother Masseo saw clearly that
Francis knew his heart of hearts;
Also that God really did direct
Francis with Divine Wisdom.
Praise to Christ. Amen.

XII

Brother Masseo's Humility

St. Francis needed to make sure of
Brother Masseo's humility;
   Because Masseo had obvious gifts and graces,
   he could become proud.
         But Francis wanted him
         to grow from virtue to virtue.
So Francis, living with his companions,
saintly in every way,
asked Brother Masseo in the presence of the others,
   "Your companions exercise the grace of
   meditation and prayer;
   You have the grace to preach God's Word
   to the great benefit of people.
   So that your friends have enough time
   to meditate,
   you must serve as
         door keeper,
         alms distributor,
         and as cook.
   While the rest of us eat,
         you will eat outside
         so you can greet visitors with blessings
         and meet all the needs of those who come.
            Do these assignments in holy obedience."
Brother Masseo pulled his hood over his lowered head,
and obeyed orders faithfully for many days.
   However, the enlightened consciences of his friends
   made them feel very badly.
   Brother Massco was a godly man.
   (More than they!)

Yet Brother Masseo shouldered everyone's
burdens.
The friars as one person
talked to Francis:
"Please divide the work equally;
Our consciences won't permit
Brother Masseo's hard labor."
Hearing this request,
Francis said Yes to their counsel,
then talked to Brother Masseo:
"Your friends want to help you,
so we'll divide tasks equally."
Brother Masseo responded with humble patience:
"Whatever you say —
all or part of the work —
I will take as God's assignment."
Then Francis saw both
the love of the friars and
the humility of Brother Masseo.
At this, Francis preached a wonderful sermon
on genuine humility,
teaching this:
The greater God's gifts
the greater our humility must be,
because God turns His back on
virtues housed in pride.
After the sermon,
he divided the tasks
with great love.
We praise Christ. Amen.

XIII

Spreading the Gospel, and the Gift of Poverty

That unusual servant and follower of Christ,
St. Francis,
wanted to be just like Jesus.
 The Gospels say Christ sent His disciples
 two by two to cities He would visit.
   Imitating Christ,
   St. Francis called together his own twelve
   to send them everywhere to preach.
 Aiming to set a true example,
 St. Francis did what Jesus did
 — he went out first,
  practicing what he asked others to do.
   So having assigned the twelve to go out,
   Francis and Masseo went elsewhere
   — to France.
Entering a town very hungry,
the two men begged for food
in God's name (as the Rule Book ordered).
 St. Francis begged on one street,
 Brother Masseo on another.
  But Francis,
  a small man,
  not very imposing,
  got only a bit of dry bread.
   Brother Masseo, a big man,
   and handsome too,
   got lots of bread, including a whole loaf.
 After begging, the two met
 on the edge of town
 to eat by a sparkling fountain
 near a beautiful slab of stone for a table

to put their food on.
St. Francis noticed Masseo's nicer pieces of bread;
this made him very happy:
    "Oh Brother Masseo,
    we're certainly not worthy of
    such a grand meal!"
Francis said that sentence over and again;
Brother Masseo replied,
"My dear teacher,
Why do you call poverty a treasure?
Why say our lack is precious?
We have no tablecloth,
    no knife,
    no board to cut on,
    no dish,
    no home,
    no table,
    no servants."
St. Francis said,
    "What is great treasure?
    When we have nothing put together by people,
    but all done by Providence —
    like the bread we begged,
        the nice looking stone table,
        the sparkling fountain.
    This explains our need to ask God for
        this holy treasure we call poverty,
        this splendid treasure God provides;
            it will make us love Him completely."
After these comments,
    they prayed;
    then eating the bread
    and drinking the water,
        they got up
        and started for France.
Arriving at a church,
St. Francis said,
    "Let's go in to worship."
St. Francis knelt behind the altar;

 49

God came to him
  and set his spirit on fire
  with love for holy poverty.
   Looking at his face and mouth,
    one seemed to see flames come from him.
Walking to Brother Masseo,
he cried out loud three times,
  "Oh! Oh! Oh! Come here, Brother Masseo."
At the third time,
   Francis' breath
    elevated Brother Masseo into the air
    and thrust him the distance
    one could throw a spear.
Brother Masseo could hardly believe what happened.
Later he told the twelve,
  "When the saint's breath lifted me,
  when he hurled me so gently,
   my soul knew only peace and beauty;
   I experienced the Holy Spirit's comfort
   — I've known nothing like it
    before or since."
After this event,
 St. Francis said to Brother Masseo,
 "Let us go to Rome
  to the tombs of St. Peter and St. Paul
  to pray for the treasure called 'the greatest poverty.'
  We could never be worthy of
  such treasure,
  for it's a heavenly virtue
  which puts earthly things into perspective
  and removes the soul's hindrances
  so we can readily be united to God.
  It will make our earthbound souls
  capable of talking the language of heaven and angels.
  This virtue went with Christ to the cross,
        to the tomb,
        to the resurrection,
        to the ascension.

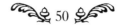

This allows our souls to rise to heaven,
and protects our humility and love.
  So let's pray in the spirit of the Apostles
  who loved 'greatest poverty' like a priceless pearl,
  that Jesus will give us the grace
  really to love this poverty,
    to observe it carefully,
    to live as true and humble disciples."
Talking like this,
they came to Rome
and entered the Church of St. Peter.
  There Francis prayed in an obscure corner;
  Brother Masseo prayed in another quiet corner.
    They stayed there a long time,
    talking to God fervently and with tears.
      Then Peter and Paul appeared to Francis:
        "Because you want so much
        to serve Christ as His Apostles did,
        Jesus sent us to say
        you have your request;
        God gives it to you and
        to your followers.
        You have poverty
          in its most complete form.
        Moreover, whoever follows perfect poverty
        will live happily forever in heaven.
        God will bless you and your followers."
      After saying this,
        Peter and Paul disappeared,
        leaving Francis in great comfort.
St. Francis got up from his knees
to ask Brother Masseo if God told him something.
  "No," he replied.
  Then Francis shared his vision and message
  from Peter and Paul.
      Great joy filled Francis and Masseo;
      they decided to return to
      the Valley of Spoleto,
      giving up France for now.

XIV

Christ Appears to St. Francis and His Brothers

During the beginning days of the Order,
St. Francis brought his friends together
to talk about Christ.
Under inspiration,
Francis told one of the friars
to talk about God,
letting the Spirit direct the words.
The friar obeyed Francis,
speaking with wonder about God.
Then, Francis told him to be quiet
so someone else could speak.
The other friar spoke about God,
using discriminating and insightful language.
Once more, Francis said, "Stop talking
and let someone else speak."
The third friar talked about God,
unfolding deep things like the others,
all inspired by the Holy Spirit.
That the three spoke under inspiration
no one could doubt,
for Christ appeared as they spoke,
looking like a perfectly formed young person,
and giving a blessing to each of the brothers.
He put pure sweetness into their souls,
elevating them beyond themselves,
so they quite forgot the world
as if they lived in heaven.
They finally came back to themselves;
then Francis spoke:

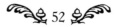

"Dear brothers,
let's thank God
who wants us to know His wisdom
even through simple people.
God gives speech to those who cannot speak;
God gives wisdom to those who are unlettered."
We praise Him. Amen.

XV

St. Clare and St. Francis Eat Together; Divine fire

When St. Francis visited Assisi,
he often visited St. Clare
to give her counsel from heaven.
She wanted very much
to eat with Francis,
    but always he said, "No."
Francis' friends knew Clare's wishes,
so they said,
    "Father, your inflexibility
    keeps poor company with God's love.
    St. Clare,
        a virgin set apart by God,
        a person loved by God,
        a woman who gave up wealth,
            who gave up the world and its pomp
            because of your preaching —
    this woman really ought to have her humble request.
    Really now, if she asked you for something greater,
        you ought to grant that,
        a natural response of your spirit."
Francis replied,
    "You believe I ought to say Yes
    to her wish?"
The friars responded,
    "Yes, Father, for she deserves it."
So St. Francis said,
    "Because you feel this way,
    so do I.

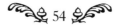

But I'm going to do something else
to add to her delight:
> We will eat at St. Mary of the Angels
> because she's been confined to St. Damian's
> for many years;
> St. Mary's will be pleasing to her.
> There she had her hair cut off
> and became Christ's bride.
> So there we shall eat together."

The day arrived.
St. Clare came with the friars
and a female companion.
> At St. Mary of the Angels,
> she greeted the Virgin Mary
> at the altar where Clare had taken
> her vows and put on the veil.

She looked all around the place
until time to eat.
Meanwhile, Francis and the friars
spread the food on the ground
(that was Francis' custom).
Time to eat came,
and St. Francis and St. Clare sat down,
and one of the friars with Clare's friend;
then all sat down.
They began to eat
and Francis talked about God
> tenderly,
> deeply,
> wonderfully;

God came down to them so much
that they sensed themselves
drawn into a heavenly rapture.
> Absorbed in God,
> they looked to Him
> with lifted hands.

Just then the people of Assisi and Bettona,

as well as surrounding towns,
saw St. Mary of the Angels,
and the forest around it,
in flames.
They ran quickly to put out the fire.
But when they got there,
they saw no flames.

    Going inside the churchyard,
    they found Francis and Clare
    and the others all seated,
    lost in meditation on God.

        Now everyone knew what the fire was:
        it came from God by a miracle,
        evidence of His love afire
        in the souls of the brothers and sisters.

            The onlookers returned to their homes
            strengthened in their spirits
            and built up in faith.

A good while after this,
Francis and Clare,
as well as the others,
came back to themselves

    stronger from the spiritual nourishment
    and needing little physical food.

        The meal over,
        Clare and the other sisters
        went back to St. Damian's.

The sisters expressed a lot of joy;
they had feared Francis would send her
to take charge of another convent.
(He had already transferred
Clare's sister, Agnes,
to serve as abbess of
the Monticelli convent in florence.)

    St. Francis once told Clare
    to stand prepared to go anywhere.

        Obediently she said,

"Father, I am prepared
to go anywhere you say."
No wonder the sisters expressed relieved joy
at seeing Clare's return.
Well, from then on,
Clare lived much consoled in the Lord.
We praise Christ. Amen.

XVI

St. Clare and Brother Silvester Reveal to St. Francis That He Should Preach; St. Francis Preaches to the Birds

Shortly after his conversion,
St. Francis, humble servant of Christ,
having gathered many friends into the Order,
    nonetheless wrestled with a concern:
        Should I pray all the time?
        Or should I preach sometimes?
        What is God's will?
His humility did not permit him
    to trust himself completely,
    nor his prayers.
So he asked others to pray about this:
    "Brother Masseo, go ask Sister Clare,
    along with her more spiritually inclined sisters,
    to ask fervently that God show me
    the better way:
        To give myself to preaching,
        Or to spend all my time praying.
    Then go to Brother Silvester
    to ask the same thing."
Before Brother Silvester joined the Order,
he saw a cross of gold pierce the sky,
wide as the earth end to end,
coming out of Francis' mouth.
    Brother Silvester talked often with God;
    God respected his devotion and holiness
    by answering his prayers.
    That's why Francis respected him so.
Brother Masseo left,

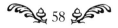

shared St. Francis' wishes with St. Clare,
then with Brother Silvester.

Immediately Brother Silvester prayed;
Immediately he got an answer from God.

"Brother Masseo,
God says you must say to Brother Francis,
'God calls you to preach
not just for yourself,
but to help others too;
God wants many saved through you.'"

Hearing that answer,
Brother Masseo went to St. Clare
to learn what God told her.

She and her friends got the same message
Brother Silvester received.

Brother Masseo went back to St. Francis
and the saint showed much love
welcoming him:

Francis washed his feet,
and also prepared food for him.

After eating,
Francis asked Masseo
to go to the woods with him,
where Francis knelt in front of him,
baring his head
and crossing his arms.

"What does my Lord
Jesus Christ
ask me to do for Him?"

Brother Masseo replied,
"Christ spoke to
Silvester,
Clare,
and Clare's sisters.

Through them He tells you
to go right into the world
preaching.

You are special to Him
not just for yourself

but even more for others."
When St. Francis heard this,
he knew Christ's will,
stood to his feet,
and said with enthusiasm,
   "We go in God's Name!"
Francis took two holy men with him,
   Brother Masseo
   and Brother Angelo.
   He and his companions started out,
   and they went with lots of motivation.
   They ignored the roadways and
   came to the hamlet of Cannara.
      St. Francis began preaching,
      first telling the singing swallows
      to quiet down till he had finished preaching.
         The swallows obeyed!
      Well! Francis preached with such enthusiasm
      that the people in the hamlet
      wanted to leave and follow Francis
      out of sheer devotion.
         Francis told them not to leave,
         not to hurry into something like that.
         More, he would instruct them
         for the salvation of their souls.
            He thought about a Third Order
            for the salvation of everybody.
Francis left these people wonderfully comforted
and in a penitent attitude.
Next he went to a spot between
Cannara and Bevagna.
      Going along in a fervent spirit
      he looked skyward to see trees by the road
      filled with countless numbers of birds.
      Captured by the wonder of the birds,
         Francis told his companions to wait
         while he went to preach
         to his sisters, the birds.
            He found a field,

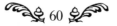

preached to some birds on the ground,
and right off, the birds in the trees
flew down to Francis and stayed
until he finished his sermon.
They wouldn't leave until
he gave the benediction.
Brother Masseo later informed Brother Jacopo da Massa
that not one bird moved
even though Francis walked among them
and let his robe brush against them.
The essence of Francis' sermon to the birds
went like this:
"My sisters,
you birds owe a lot to God;
so you must always praise Him.
He gives you
Freedom to fly in the sky;
Two and three layers of feathers,
colorful and pretty;
Food that you don't have to work for;
He taught you how to sing;
He blessed you and multiplied you;
He saved your race from death in Noah's ark;
The realm of the air He assigns you.
You don't have to plant and harvest,
yet God feeds you,
gives you rivers,
gives you fountains too,
gives you mountains and valleys for shelter,
gives you high trees for nests.
No, you don't know how to make cloth,
nor how to sew,
Yet He dresses you and yours.
He loves you very much,
He gives you many good things.
Therefore, guard against ingratitude — a sin!
Strive always to praise God!"
After the sermon,
the birds opened their beaks,

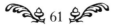

stretched their necks,
spread their wings,
bowed their heads reverently,
    showing by body and song
    that the holy Francis gave them
    great joy by his words.
St. Francis joined in their joyous praise,
    amazed at so many birds,
        at their individuality,
        at their ability to listen,
        at their love —
            and so, with great devotion,
            he praised their Creator
            for them.
After the sermon,
St. Francis
made the sign of the cross over the birds,
then told them they could go.
    The birds together pierced the heavens
    with beautiful songs,
        then arranged themselves in the pattern
        of St. Francis' sign of the cross:
            One line of birds flew eastward,
            Another stream went to the west,
            Another south,
            And still another, north —
                all the while singing
                with breath-taking beauty.
    Like the cross which St. Francis traced in the air,
        the birds went off
        singing to the four corners of the world.
    Their flight pattern told the world that
    St. Francis' preaching
    signaled a renewed preaching of the cross
    throughout the world;
        He and the friars would preach everywhere,
        like the birds who owned nothing in the world,
        but trusted themselves to God's Providence.
For all these truths we lift up praise to Christ. Amen.

XVII

A Young Friar Watches St. Francis Pray

During St. Francis' lifetime,
an especially pure and innocent lad
joined the Order.
The brothers stayed in a small place,
    so small they had to sleep on the ground.
    St. Francis once came to this place;
        In the evening after prayers,
        he went right to bed
        so he could get up in the night to pray
        while the brothers slept.
The lad determined to watch Francis
so he could see his sanctity firsthand;
    Especially he wanted to see what Francis did
    in the night after getting out of bed.
The young fellow didn't want to sleep through all that,
so he slept next to Francis,
    tied the rope around his waist
    to the rope around St. Francis' waist
    in order to come awake when Francis got up.
        Francis didn't notice the knot-tying.
But during the first sound sleep,
when all the friars really slept,
St. Francis got up;
    he discovered his cincture knotted to the lad's
    but untied it quietly enough not to wake him.
        Then Francis walked into the woods alone,
        not far from where he left them sleeping
        and where Francis went into a hut to pray.
A bit later, the young man awakened,
finding the rope undone and Francis gone away.

So he got up to look for Francis;
    finding the friary door open,
    the lad assumed Francis went to the woods,
    so naturally he went searching.
        He found the place where St. Francis prayed
        and heard voices.
            Moving closer to understand the words,
            he saw a marvelous light all around the saint;
                In the light the lad saw Christ,
                and the Virgin Mary,
                and St. John the Baptist,
                and St. John the Evangelist,
                and many angels —
                    all talking with St. Francis.
                    Well! Seeing this,
                    the young friar fainted dead away.
When the vision went away,
Francis returned to the sleeping quarters;
        But, in going, he stumbled onto the boy
        lying across his path as though dead.
            Compassionately, Francis gathered him
            in his arms,
            then put him to bed,
            as a good shepherd cares for his sheep.
Later St. Francis discovered
the lad had seen the miraculous vision;
        Francis commanded him to say nothing,
        nothing whatever so long as the saint lived.
            The boy matured by God's grace,
            devoted to St. Francis,
            and served valiantly in the Order.
                Only after Francis died
                did he tell the story to the brothers.
We praise Christ. Amen.

XVIII

St. Francis Preaches to 5,000 Friars

St. Francis,
that most faithful servant of Christ,
called all his friars —
    some 5,000 of them —
    to come to St. Mary of the Angels.
St. Dominic,
founding head of the Order of Preachers,
    also came on his way from Bologna to Rome.
    Learning of St. Francis' meeting
    in the acreage around St. Mary of the Angels,
        Dominic appeared with seven of his own friars.
Cardinal Ugolino,
a devotee of St. Francis,
also arrived.
    (St. Francis once prophesied
    the Cardinal would become Pope —
    and that eventually happened —
    he became Gregory the Ninth.)
        The Cardinal came from the
        papal court in Perugia;
            Each day he saw St. Francis
            and his brothers.
                One time the Cardinal would sing Mass,
                another time preach to the friars;
                Always he delighted in the
                spiritual fellowship of the gathering.
            Groups of sixty here,
                a hundred there,
                even three hundred another place —
                    seeing all these groups seated

just to worship,
weeping in repentance,
doing charitable things —
and doing all this in such quiet modesty
that no sound broke the silence,
brought tears to the Cardinal's eyes
and inspired him to great devotion.
"Here, in this field," he said,
"I see an army of Christ's knights."
No one in all this great crowd
told funny stories or clowned around.
But they prayed,
recited the Office,
wept for their sins,
wept for the sins of their supporters,
and talked to one another about the salvation of souls.
The encampment looked like this:
Huts made of rushes and mats;
The huts put into groupings from the different provinces.
(This explains the name of this chapter of the Order:
"The Chapter of Rushes and Mats".)
The inside of the huts looked like this:
Just the ground for beds;
Sometimes a bit of straw;
Pillows of wood or stone.
People who had a chance to see or hear about these things,
found themselves inspired to great devotion.
Well! the word got around
to the papal court at Perugia,
places around the Valley of Spoleto;
Counts and barons,
Knights, gentlemen and commoners,
Cardinals, bishops, abbots, and other clergy —
all wanted to see this saintly and humble crowd,
a larger crowd than anyone had ever seen.
They came especially to see St. Francis,
father of this big group,
who had robbed the world of first rate people,

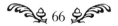

who had assembled a flock,
at once beautiful and devout,
to walk in the steps of Jesus Christ,
utterly worthy Shepherd.
St. Francis,
the holy father of those assembled,
called the friars to order with a lot of enthusiasm,
and focused their attention on God's Word.
In a strong, projected voice,
he shared the Spirit's message.
The sermon's theme?
"Sons, you and I have made some big promises;
But God promises us even bigger things!
You and I will live out our promises
with the sure knowledge that God will be
true to us,
even if we have to wait a bit.
In this world, pleasures
live only a little while;
In the next world,
punishment lasts forever.
Suffering here goes on only briefly;
Glory in the next life never ends!"
Well, Brother Francis talked on that theme
with rich devotion,
with comfort to all,
exhorting all to obedience and respect
for the Church and
for doing acts of charity.
More! Brother Francis exhorted everyone to
worship God with adoration,
live patiently in bad times,
live modestly in good times,
live always in purity,
live with the chastity of angels,
live in peace and harmony with others,
God,
and one's own conscience.

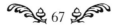

Also to honor poverty,
    an instrument of holiness.
St. Francis went on:
    "Let me charge you all in Holy Obedience to
        Focus not on what you eat,
                drink,
                or wear,
      But on prayer and praise of God,
        trusting Him to care for your body,
        because He cares for you."
Everyone listened to Francis' sermon
and his commands,
with joy in their hearts and
    on their faces.
When Francis finished the sermon,
    everyone turned to prayer.
St. Dominic witnessed all this
and stood in amazement at
St. Francis' command;
Actually, Dominic thought Francis imprudent,
for how could such a crowd ignore the care of their bodies?
    But Christ, Blessed Shepherd,
    demonstrated His care of the people
    (He *does* show special care of the poor):
    He enkindled the people of
              Perugia,
              Spoleto,
              Foligno,
              Spello,
              Assisi,
        and other nearby towns,
           to bring food and drink
           to this sacred gathering.
Men came with donkeys,
        horses,
        and carts
           filled with bread and wine,
              beans and cheese,

every good food for Christ's
hungry poor.
Men also brought table coverings,
containers,
dishes,
cups or tumblers,
anything and everything necessary.
Those capable of bringing or serving more
found themselves especially fulfilled.
No wonder knights, barons and nobles,
who came at first to see what was going on,
now stayed to serve the friars in humble respect.
St. Dominic, observing all this,
recognized God at work
and now admitted he had misjudged Francis.
In humility, he knelt to admit his error;
then said,
"Clearly God takes special care of
these poor and little people;
I hadn't realized that before.
Beginning now,
I take the poverty vow;
I command my own friars to do the same!"
St. Dominic was edified by St. Francis' faith
and by the holy obedience of such a huge
and well-ordered gathering;
And also by seeing God's abundant generosity.
Well, at this same chapter meeting of the Order,
St. Francis learned that many friars
wore iron vests and chains
underneath their clothes.
Some monks got sick,
died even;
Many could not concentrate
to pray.
St. Francis had the good sense to
require all iron undergarments be
brought to him.

500 iron vests,
many armbands,
also stomach chains —
all this made a small hill!
St. Francis left them right there.
Now then, the chapter meeting came to an end,
St. Francis strengthening the men with courage,
teaching them how to do good things,
showing them how to guard against sin
in an evil world,
sending them back to their provinces
with God's blessing and his own,
putting joy in their hearts.
In praise of Jesus Christ. Amen.

XIX

St. Francis' Eyes, and the Productive Vineyard

St. Francis' eyes got worse and worse.
Ugolino, Cardinal Protector of the Order,
because he cared for Francis very much,
wrote him:
    "Do go to Rieti where you can
    talk to first rate eye doctors."
Francis got the letter,
then went to St. Damian's
    to comfort Clare
    (a very devoted bride of Christ);
After that, Francis aimed to see
the Cardinal.
    But that night,
    Francis' eyes got still worse;
        now he couldn't even see light.
        Unable to leave,
        he stayed at St. Damian's.
            Clare made a little hut of reeds
            so he could be by himself.
            But he couldn't rest because
                his eyes hurt and
                rats crawled over him all the time,
                day and night.
During this seemingly unending pain and misery,
Francis thought about his condition,
and came to believe God sent this scourge
as punishment for his sins.
    He praised God from his depths:
        "I deserve this,
        my God,

and oh so much more!
My Lord Jesus Christ,
my Good Shepherd,
Your sufferings,
    Your physical pain,
        Your mercy — in spite of your own misery —
        to unworthy sinners
            leads me to ask,
                'Will You help me,
                Your small lamb,
                to exercise grace and strength
                to allow no illness,
                    no suffering,
                    no pain
                to separate me from You?'"
After this prayer,
a voice right out of heaven said,
    "Francis, answer this question for Me:
        If the earth turned to gold;
        If seas, rivers, fountains
            turned to balsam;
        If mountains, hills, rocks
            turned to precious stones;
        If you found an even greater treasure,
            like gold surpasses earth,
                balsam surpasses water,
                gems surpass mountains and rocks;
        If this surpassing treasure
        I gave you in exchange for
        your problem,
            wouldn't you feel
            excited joy and real happiness?"
St. Francis responded,
    "Master,
    I don't deserve
    such a wonderful treasure."
God spoke again:
    "Be very happy, Francis;

The treasure is Life Eternal.
I've kept it for you;
I now give it to you.
Your afflictions symbolize
My promise of this
wonderful treasure."
St. Francis, now filled with the news of glorious promise,
his voice revealing excited joy,
said to his companion,
"Let's go see the Cardinal!"
But before he left,
he offered encouraging words to Clare —
words holy and strengthening —
then he went humbly in the direction of Rieti.
Near Rieti,
a lot of people came out to him,
so he decided to skirt the town
and go to a church about two miles away.
When all the people discovered the church,
they flocked in great numbers to see him.
The people picked the grapes,
ruining the priest's vineyard;
the priest felt angry,
now sorry he allowed Francis into his church!
God told Francis about
the priest's feelings;
so Francis called for the pastor,
then asked,
"How many donkey-loads of wine
does your vineyard yield in the best year?"
The priest said, "Twelve."
Francis asked,
"Would I ask too much,
would I tax your patience,
by staying here several days?
I rest well here.
For the love of Christ and poor little me,
let the people take all the grapes;

> I promise in Christ's name,
> He will reward you with twenty donkey-loads."
> (Francis said all this so he could stay
> to help the people;
> Many left intoxicated with God's love,
> forgetting their everyday cares.)
> The priest trusted Francis' promise
> and freely told the people
> to help themselves to the grapes.
> Would you believe the miracle?
> Though the people stripped the vines,
> except for a few clusters,
> at harvest time the priest
> put the few clusters in the press —
> he did this by faith in Francis' promise —
> and lo! twenty donkey-loads of excellent wine!

This miracle shows us how
God used St. Francis to teach how,
Even as stripped vines
can produce lots of wine,
so Christians stripped of good by sin
can yield beautiful fruit
by repentance.
We praise Christ. Amen.

XX

A Struggling Friar Comes to Commitment

A young man from a refined family
joined St. Francis' Order.
  But in a few days
  the devil suggested negative feelings
  about the clothes he wore:
      "Such an old sack I'm wearing!
      Look at these sleeves,
      and this cowl;
        the length of the cassock, too,
        and its coarseness!
      It's all terribly unbearable."
  Then he grew in his dislike for the Order itself.
      "Why not go back to the world?"
      he asked himself.
The night came when he would leave the Order;
but he had to walk in front of the sanctuary altar.
  His upbringing called for
    kneeling in serious reverence,
    baring his head,
    crossing his arms —
        all in front of the altar,
        honoring the Presence of Christ.
He did all this.
But, while kneeling,
    suddenly he sensed the elevation of his spirit
    and he saw a most beautiful vision:
        Countless saints in procession,
        walking in pairs,
        dressed magnificently in expensive cloth,
        their hands and faces glowing like the sun.

As they walked,
    they sang like angels.
Two wore richer looking clothes than the others;
    they radiated love.
(The young man looked in amazement.)
Toward the end of the long line,
    he could see someone
    clothed in such glory —
    well, as if just knighted,
    honored more than the others.
You can believe the young gentleman
looked at this vision in utter amazement,
    but did not know its meaning.
    He felt checked about asking its meaning,
    so he simply knelt in blissful wonder.
    Yet at about the end of the procession,
courage took command of his spirit —
    he ran to the last saints in the procession
    and in awe and deep respect, asked,
        "Friends, would you please
        be good enough to identify
        all these extraordinary men
        in this awesome procession?"
They replied,
    "Son,
    we want you to know
    we are Friars Minor
    walking into Paradise in all its glory."
Then the young gentleman asked,
    "Will you identify the two persons
    more radiant than the others?"
They replied,
    "Saint Francis and Saint Anthony.
    The last one you saw died recently
    and he is a saintly brother;
        he fought courageously against temptations
        and stuck it out to the end.
        God is leading him in great victory

to Paradise in all its glory.
All these beautiful clothes we wear?
    Given us by God
    in place of the coarse habits
    we wore for the Order day after day.
And the radiating love you see?
    Given us by God
    as reward for humble penance,
        holy poverty,
        obedience,
        chastity —
    all these disciplines
    we observed to the end.
So, dear son,
    It's really not hard to wear St. Francis' sack
    because it bears fruit.
You see,
    to wear St. Francis' sack
    because you love Christ
    and hate the world
    and put down the flesh
    and fight courageously against evil —
well! you, with us, will wear
special clothes and shine in glory."
After hearing all this,
the young man came to himself once more
and experienced great comfort from the vision.
    He threw off his temptations,
        confessed his error
            both to his superior and
            to his fellow friars.
From this point on
    he wanted hard-as-nails penance,
        and unrefined clothes.
He passed away as a member of the Order,
leaving the perfume of sanctity.
We praise Christ. Amen.

XXI

St. Francis Delivers Gubbio From a Fierce Wolf

When St. Francis lived in Gubbio,
a big wolf, terrifying because ferocious,
actually ate people as well as animals.
    Townsfolk lived with enormous fear
    because the wolf often appeared in Gubbio.
        When the wolf came,
        the people emerged from their homes
        armed and ready to fight.
            Yet! people felt helpless,
            especially when someone faced the wolf alone.
            Not surprisingly,
            people stayed home,
            not even leaving the town.
St. Francis heard all about this,
took pity on the people,
and made up his mind to see the wolf,
    even though everyone told him not to.
    Under the sign of the cross,
    Francis took some friends
    and placed his trust fully in God.
        When his friends,
        having left Gubbio,
        got afraid to go further,
            St. Francis went on by himself,
            following the wolf's path
                to his place.
                Actually many people watched
                while the wolf came up to Francis,
                the wolf's mouth open and ready to eat him!
                    Francis made the sign of the cross in the air,

then said,
        "Brother Wolf,
        come to me.
        In Christ's Name,
        you will hurt no one,
        myself included."
    With the sign of the cross,
    the wolf shut his mouth and stood still.
    Then, like a lamb,
    he lay down at Francis' feet.
St. Francis talked to the wolf:
    "Brother Wolf,
    you've harmed and hurt people without God's permission.
        You've killed animals;
        you've killed people,
            made in God's image.
        Well! You deserve to go to the gallows,
        thieving, murdering criminal that you are.
            All these people are your enemies,
            wanting the worst to happen to you.
        But, Brother Wolf, I want to
            make peace between you and them,
            put a stop to your bad behavior,
            watch them forgive you of everything —
                then neither persons nor dogs
                will want to torture you anymore."
All through talking,
St. Francis watched the wolf
accept the offer of peace;
    The wolf signaled approval with his body,
                                tail,
                                ears and
                                lowered head.
At this, St. Francis said,
    "Brother Wolf, because you agree to peace,
    I shall have the people feed you
    as long as you live;
        You will never go hungry —

in the past you did bad things
due to hunger.
With this gracious promise,
I want you never to hurt any person
or animal again.
Do you promise?"
The bowed head of the wolf
indicated his affirmative answer.
Then Francis pressed the wolf,
"Brother Wolf, give me your word
so that I can believe you completely."
The wolf answered by lifting his paw
when St. Francis offered his hand;
Actually, the wolf put his paw into
St. Francis' hand with assuring gentleness
showing the wolf's definite agreement.
So Francis ordered the wolf to come to him
to sign a treaty of peace
in God's name.
The wolf followed obediently,
as gentle as a lamb.
The citizens watched in amazed wonder.
This news spread everywhere in the town;
everyone —
men and women,
young and old,
children and grown-ups —
they all came to the town's square
to see Francis and the wolf together.
Francis, standing before such a crowd,
preached, saying things such as
God allows calamities because of sins;
Hell's flames will last eternally,
and therefore pose a more dangerous threat
than the wolf's fury,
for a wolf can kill only the body.
So! See things in perspective:
Hell's mouth should put a lot more fear into us

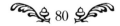

than the wolf's mouth,
	a mouth much smaller than hell's!
Turn to God, dearest friends;
Repent and do penance so that
	God will free you from the wolf now
	and from hell's fires in the future.
After the sermon, St. Francis commented,
	"Listen, dear friends,
	Brother Wolf standing here
	promises me on his word
	he will live at peace with all of you.
He will do you no harm
	if you meet his daily needs.
I myself pledge his strict observance of
	the peace treaty."
All the people promised to take care of the wolf
on a daily basis.
	Before everybody, St. Francis said to the wolf:
	"Do you, Brother Wolf, promise
	to keep the peace?
	Do you refuse to harm or scare anyone,
		people or animals?"
The wolf knelt, lowered his head, with meekness
	wiggled his ears and tail,
	his way of saying, Yes.
St. Francis pressed the wolf:
"Brother Wolf,
	Just as you showed me your Yes
	outside the walls of Gubbio,
	now give all these people your Yes
	so they will know for sure you will not betray them."
The wolf lifted his paw
and placed it in St. Francis' hand.
	Such rejoicing on the part of the people!
	They rejoiced out of respect for the saint,
		at the unusual character of the miracle,
		and in gratitude for the peace pact.
	Well, why not praise God!

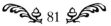

They now enjoyed freedom from the cruel attacks
of the wolf.
The wolf lived two years in Gubbio,
gently going from house to house.
He harmed no one;
no one harmed him.
The people fed him courteously;
not even farm dogs barked at him!
When the wolf died of old age,
the people actually grieved,
because the wolf's appearance
reminded them of the great blessing
of the saintly Francis.
In praise of Christ. Amen.

XXII

St. Francis and the Turtle Doves

A young man caught some doves
and made his way to market to sell them.
    On the way,
        he ran into St. Francis,
            who always showed great love
            for helpless animals.
    Francis, his eyes filled with compassion,
    said to the lad,
        "Dear young fellow,
        do give me those innocent doves,
        compared in the Bible to
            humble,
                gentle,
                    pure persons.
        Don't let the birds go into
        cruel hands,
        hands which could kill them."
On the spot,
the young fellow gave all his birds to
St. Francis.
    Francis held them in his lap,
    then talked to them:
        "My sisters,
            sweet,
            harmless,
                pure turtle doves,
        Why did you allow the lad to
        capture you?
        Never mind,
            I will save you from death.

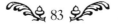

Do make nests,
      have young birds,
         multiply yourselves
            just like your Creator wishes."
St. Francis himself made nests for them.
   The doves lived in them,
      laid their eggs in them,
      had their young in them —
         the friars watched all this.
   The doves, tame and gentle,
acted as if Francis and the friars
had raised them.
      Actually, they did not leave
      until Francis said they could —
         when he did, he gave them
         his blessing.
St. Francis said to the lad
who gave the birds to him,
   "One day, my son,
   you will join our Order
   as a friar,
   lovingly serving Christ."
      That's exactly what happened:
         The young fellow joined the Order,
         became a brother,
         and lived like a saint until he died.
In praise of Christ. Amen.

XXIII

St. Francis and the Angry Friar

One day at prayer in the friary at Portiuncula,
St. Francis saw
    (by divine revelation)
    the friary surrounded and attacked
    by an army of devils.
        Not one devil could enter;
        the friars lived holy lives, and the
        devils therefore found no place to enter.
        Yet they persisted.
            One friar got angry at another,
            and privately thought about accusing him
            to take revenge.
                This opened the door and
                a devil came into the friary
                to cling to the angry brother.
Well! Francis, guarding shepherd of the flock,
called in the angry friar
so the wolf wouldn't eat the lamb.
    Francis ordered the friar to
    cough up the poison in his soul
    (the anger against his brother)
    which allowed the devil to come in.
        Horror gripped the friar! (Francis saw through him!)
        He confessed his sin;
        He acknowledged his fault;
        He humbly requested mercy and penance.
            The sin forgiven and penance granted,
            the devil made tracks and left him.

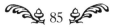

Naturally the brother thanked God,
for his shepherd had helped him get free.
He returned to the others,
the spiritual surgery successful,
and decidedly grew in holiness.
In praise of Christ. Amen.

XXIV

St. Francis' Desire to Convert the Sultan

St. Francis,
    zealous for the faith of Christ, and
    wanting martyrdom,
        took a sea voyage with twelve friends,
        the holiest of friars,
        to see the Sultan of Babylon.
            When they arrived in the land of the Saracens,
            where crossing the nation's borders
            (guarded by cruel fellows)
                meant sure death,
                    God did not let Francis and his friends die.
                    Men whipped them,
                        tied them, then
                        took them to the Sultan.
When St. Francis stood in the presence of the Sultan,
he preached Christ with the Spirit's anointing;
    Francis, so zealous was he,
    would not have resisted even fire
    for the sake of Jesus Christ.
The response of the Sultan?
    A great attraction for Francis;
    Respect for his faithfulness;
    Equal respect for his contempt of the world.
The Sultan could see that Francis
    wanted nothing for himself,
        though very poor, and
    concerned himself only with suffering for
        the faith.
That's why the Sultan listened to Francis,
even begged him to come often,

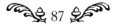

giving him and his friends
freedom to preach anywhere any time.
He guaranteed them perfect safety.
So with this permission,
St. Francis sent his men by pairs
to several Saracen areas
to preach faith in Christ.
He, with one other friar,
walked down a road
until they came to an inn where they could rest.
In that place a beautiful but corrupt
woman tempted Francis.
St. Francis said,
"Alright, let's go to bed."
She took him to her room.
In holy zest he stripped,
lay on the burning fireplace, and
invited her to lie with him.
He lay there a long time,
but suffered no burns,
yet smiled!
When she saw that,
she grew frightened
and suffered a pricked conscience
in the presence of this miracle!
Well, she repented thoroughly,
came to conversion by
faith in Christ,
and became so holy
that many were saved
through her example.
After some time, Francis saw
he could do no more good among the Saracens;
so, guided by the Spirit,
he called his friends to return to the faithful.
Once they all got back together,
he went to the Sultan to say good-bye.
Then the Sultan said,

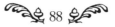 88

"I really want to put my faith in Christ;
but just now I cannot, lest my people
        murder me,
        kill you,
        destroy your friends.
Because I know you can do a lot of good,
because I must make big decisions,
        I don't want to see you or myself die.
But give me information about
        how to be saved.
        I'll do whatever you say."
Then Francis said,
    "Your lordship,
        I must go now,
        but when I return home,
        and by God's grace have come to heaven
        after death,
        if God wills, I will send you
            two of my friars.
            They will baptize you in Christ's name
            and you will be saved,
                just as my Lord Jesus Christ told me.
    In the meantime,
        stay away from anything that
            hinders grace
            so when it comes
            you will find yourself open to it."
    The Sultan did as he promised.
After this conversation,
St. Francis and his holy friends left.
    Some years later, Francis died and his soul went to God.
    The Sultan got sick.
    Anticipating St. Francis' promise,
    the Sultan put guards at some of the country's
    border places.
        He said that if two friars,
        dressed like St. Francis,
        came to the country's border,

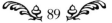

they must go immediately to the Sultan.
At that very time,
     St. Francis appeared to two friars
     and told them to go quickly to the Sultan
     and lead him to salvation
     (as Francis had promised).
So the friars started immediately,
crossed the sea,
and the guards took them to the Sultan.
When the Sultan saw them,
his heart filled up with joy.
     "I couldn't possibly doubt God sent His servants
     for my salvation,
     so that St. Francis' promise,
     made by God's own revelation,
     would come true."
When the friars instructed him
the Sultan experienced the new birth and
baptism into Christ.
Then he died of his sickness
but his soul was saved —
all because of Francis' prayers.
In praise of Christ Jesus. Amen.

XXV

St. Francis Helps a Leper

St. Francis,
genuine disciple of Christ,
worked with all his might to imitate his Master.
    So very often
    when Francis asked God to heal a body,
    the soul found healing too,
    just as in Jesus' ministry.
        That's why he helped lepers
        with such enthusiasm;
        And he told his friars,
        wherever they went in the world,
        to help lepers for the love of Christ,
        who Himself wanted to be treated like a leper.
One day near St. Francis' living quarters,
friars caring for ill people,
including lepers,
tried to help an absolutely obnoxious leper,
    impatient,
    maddening,
    muleheaded.
        No wonder everyone believed him
        possessed of a devil:
            He swore at people who tried to serve him;
            He behaved like he spoke;
            Worse, he cursed Christ and the Virgin Mary.
                No one wanted to take care of him!
                    Friars would have cared for him,
                    even willingly listened to curses
                        directed at them;
                    But curses against Christ and Mary?

— That they couldn't condone.
Before abandoning him, however,
the brothers felt they must inform Francis.
After Francis was told,
he went with them to the evil man,
walked right up to the leper
with this greeting:
    "Very dear brother,
    God gives you peace."
The leper grumbled a reply:
    "What do you mean —
    God gives me peace?
    How?
    God robbed me of peace,
            of all I owned,
            of my personhood
                — I'm smelly and putrid!"
St. Francis replied:
    "Exercise patience;
    Sickness can be God's gift
    opening us to salvation;
    Illness has enormous merit
    when endured calmly."
The leprous man answered:
    "How can I calmly endure pain
    day and night?
    I'm not only imprisoned by this disease,
    I'm made worse by your friars
    — you directed them to help me —
    who don't care for me as they ought."
At this, St. Francis,
who knew by God's voice that
the man had an evil spirit,
prayed earnestly for him.
    After interceding for him,
    Francis returned to the man:
        "My son,
        Since the others don't suit you,

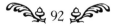

I myself want to take care of you."
The diseased fellow accepted Francis' offer;
then asked,
    "But what can you do for me
    the others couldn't?"
St. Francis said,
    "Whatever you want me to do,
    I will do."
The leprous man replied,
    "I want a complete bath,
    because my body gives off an odor
    I cannot stand."
St. Francis went into action:
    He heated water;
    He put nice smelling herbs in the water;
    He took the man's clothes off
    (while another friar heated more water);
    He washed him with his own hands.
Now miracles took place:
    Wherever Francis touched the poor man,
        the leprosy went away;
    Wherever Francis touched the poor man,
        healthy flesh appeared;
    While the flesh healed,
        the soul healed.
The healed leper
    had great sorrow for his sins.
    Remorse gripped him;
    weeping expressed his regret.
      So while the body healed
      the soul healed too;
          his sins were washed away by
          repentance
          and tears.
      When completely healed
      in body and in spirit,
      he accepted blame
      and cried out,

"Woe to myself;
I deserve hell
for my offenses and injuries
against the friars,
for my stubbornness and blasphemy
against God."
For fifteen days the healed man wept,
terribly sorry for his sins,
pleading for mercy from God,
making complete confession to a priest.
When Francis saw this true miracle,
he knew God did it through him;
he thanked God and
then went a long way away,
for humility motivated him to
stay away from all adulation;
In all he did,
Francis aimed to honor God,
to glorify Him,
and not himself.
Later it seemed to please God
to allow the man who had leprosy
to fall ill with another disease;
During fifteen days of penance,
armed with the Church's sacraments,
the good man died a sacred death.
After going to paradise
he appeared to St. Francis at prayer;
He said,
"You remember me, don't you?"
Francis replied,
"Tell me who you are."
He answered,
"I am the leper
whom the Blessed Christ
healed through you;
This is my day to
begin eternal life.

I want to thank you and God.
God bless you in spirit and body;
God bless your words and actions,
  because many will come to salvation
  through you.
Know this:
  Not a day will pass
  without holy angels,
  and saints, too,
  thanking God for the sacred work
  you and your Order do
  here and there in the world.
So accept heaven's comfort;
Thank God.
I pray His blessing to rest upon you."
With these words he entered fully into eternal life,
and St. Francis sensed the consolation of heaven's comfort.
In praise of Christ, the Blessed One. Amen.

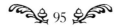

XXVI

Three Thieves Become Friars;
One of Them is Shown Heaven and Hell

St. Francis,
travelling one day
in the district of
Borgo San Sepolcro,
    passed through the village of Monte Casale.
    A young nobleman,
    protected by his wealth,
    approached Francis:
        "Father, I want very much
        to become one of your friars."
    Francis responded:
        "Young man,
        luxury has sheltered you;
        Do you honestly believe
        you could adjust
        to the rough and meager life
        of a friar?"
    The young fellow replied:
        "Father, aren't you and your men like me?
        If you can all put up with a hard life,
        so can I,
        by God's grace."
Well, Brother Francis really liked this reply,
so he gave the young man his blessing,
then received him into the Order right away,
naming him Brother Angelo.
    The youth demonstrated such graces,
    after only a short time,
    that Francis put him in charge

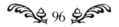

of the Friary at Monte Casale.
About this time,
the district suffered from three
well-known robbers;
they did a lot of bad things everywhere.
     One day these miserable fellows
     appeared at the friary;
     They asked Brother Angelo for food.
          He, though, scolded them harshly:
               "You robbers and heartless murderers,
               You have no conscience
                    about taking what others earn by hard work;
               Proud and irresponsible,
                    you would even take
                    what's given to God's servants!
               You certainly don't respect the
               earth that gives you life;
                    Nor do you reverence people
                    or the God who created you.
               So get out of here; and don't return."
The robbers left with troubled minds
and full of bitterness.
St. Francis appeared about this time
with some bread and a bit of wine
which he and his friends had begged.
     When Brother Angelo told him
     about driving off the thieves,
     St. Francis rebuked him straight from the shoulder:
          "Such a cruel way to handle them!
          Kindness brings sinners to God
          far better than harsh words.
               That's why our Lord and Master,
               whose Good News we follow,
               tells us the healthy don't need the doctor,
                    but sick people do;
               More! He came to call sinners,
                    not those who are good.
               Now do you see why Jesus

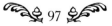

often ate with bad people?
The way you acted and negated love
went against the Gospel;
therefore you must do the following:
Take this basket of bread
and this container of wine;
Go find the robbers,
even if you have to go
over hill and dale.
Tell them the bread and wine
come from me;
Kneel in front of them
and humbly confess your sin,
your cruel sin.
Plead with them for me
to stop their wicked ways,
to honor God and
to quit offending their neighbors.
If they say Yes to this,
promise to meet all their needs,
giving them something to eat
and something to drink.
When you have done all this,
return here."
Brother Angelo set out to do what Francis ordered;
Francis began to pray,
asking God to soften the robbers' hearts,
to make them want to repent.
The obeying friar caught up with the robbers,
gave them bread and wine;
he did what Francis ordered.
This made God happy because
while the thieves ate and drank,
they said to one another,
"Alas!
We're terrible people,
wretches;
We deserve hell.

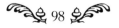 98

We rob,
    beat and
    hurt people,
    even murder.
Though we do terrible things,
we have no remorse,
    no bad conscience,
    no fear of God.
But this good friar came to us;
More! He apologized for
    his harsh words justly spoken.
    He confessed his fault with humility.
    He even brought bread and wine,
      and a remarkably generous promise
      from Father Francis.
Well, these friars show what it means to be a saint.
They deserve paradise;
we deserve hell,
    the pains of eternal damnation
    and daily additions to our pain.
    We've committed lots of sins.
    Can God give the likes of us mercy?"
These comments were made by one of the robbers;
one of the other two said,
    "You speak clear truth;
    But what can we do?"
The first thief replied,
    "Let's go to St. Francis;
    let's see if he offers any hope at all
    for God to forgive our sins.
    We will do whatever he says,
      for we may succeed in avoiding
      hell's pains."
This idea seemed good to the others,
and together they went to St. Francis:
    "Father, how could God give us mercy?
    We've done horrible things.
    Can you see any hope for us?

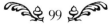

Will God accept us in His mercy?
We will do anything you say;
we will do penance too."
St. Francis responded kindly,
with love,
even comforting them with examples of conversion.
He gave them assurance of the endless mercy of God.
More! He told them that the greater the sin,
the greater the mercy of God!
The Gospel said that,
St. Paul announced that,
"Christ came to save sinners."
What St. Francis said and taught
gripped the robbers;
They said a firm No to the devil
and all his works.
St. Francis took them into the Order
and they started following through on their repentance.
Two lived only a short while
after their conversion;
Then they went to Paradise.
The third survived,
thought about his sins
and made penance for them by
fasting three days a week
(bread and water only),
going barefoot,
possessing only one habit,
never sleeping past Matins.
— All this he did for fifteen years.
About the time Francis died,
the friar had done his penances for many years.
One night after Matins,
he couldn't resist sleep and couldn't pray.
He went to his bed and
there had a vision
which began as soon as his head hit the pillow.
He felt himself carried away

to a very high mountain.
A terrible ravine opened before him,
both sides revealing sharp crags
and projecting ledges.
        Such a scene!
An angel led him,
then pushed him over the side;
    He hurtled down,
    bounding from rock to rock,
                boulder to boulder.
    finally he landed at the
    bottom of the precipice,
        totally broken,
        terribly torn.
            There, the angel-guide talked to him
            in his intolerable situation:
                "Get up, for you must go
                a long way yet."
The friar answered:
    "You stupid and cruel person!
    Already you made me fall;
    already I'm nearly dead.
    Yet you tell me to get up."
Now the angel touched him,
healing all his limbs.
Next the angel showed him a wide piece of land
    on which the friar saw sharp stones,
                    thorns and briars.
    The angel told him
    to cross the land barefoot,
    to walk until he reached the end.
    The friar did that,
        suffering all the way.
        Then the angel ordered him
        to enter a fiery furnace;
        that, too, he had to do.
The poor man spoke again:
    "Dear me!

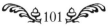

101

How cruelly you treat me,
even though you serve as my guide.
I'm near death after the
agonizing crossing;
Why can't I rest now?
No, I must go into the fire."
He looked around to see many devils,
each with forks;
They poked him
until he got into the furnace.
Inside he saw an acquaintance
engulfed in flames.
"You poor fellow,
how did you get here?"
He replied:
"Keep going;
you will see my wife (your cousin)
who will tell you why we're here."
So he walked on to see his relative,
also engulfed in flame,
enclosed in a fiery prison.
"Dear cousin,
how on earth did you get into
this terrible place?"
She answered:
"When St. Francis predicted
the big famine,
my husband and I told lies
about our grain and wheat;
We sold it as if it weighed
more than it really did.
That's why we're shut up in this fire box."
Then the angel-guide shoved the monk
out of the furnace:
"Get ready to go on a terrible trip,
a trip that you must take."
Complaining, he said,
"You relentless guide!

Can't you pity me?
Though the furnace scorched me,
you insist on this dangerous, miserable journey."
The angel, touching him,
brought new life and energy to him.
The angel took him to a bridge,
crossable only under terrible danger,
Wobbly and narrow,
very slippery with no handrails;
Under it a frightening river
filled with snakes,
monsters,
and scorpions —
all giving off foul smells.
The angel insisted he cross the bridge.
The friar asked,
"How can I cross it
without plunging into
the dangerous water below?"
The angel then said,
"Follow me,
putting your feet where mine go,
then you will cross without harm."
So the angel went first;
the friar followed.
They reached the center of the bridge;
then the angel flew away.
Sizing up his dilemma,
and knowing only God could help him now,
he knelt,
held tightly to the bridge,
then gave himself to God
with his whole heart,
with weeping,
and with pleas for mercy.
Ending his prayer,
he thought he grew wings.
He waited joyfully,

hoping wings would come
for flying after the angel.
    After a while he tried to fly,
    so driven was he to get away;
    but the immature wings
    could not carry him, so
    he and his wings fell onto the bridge.
He now gripped the bridge,
and once more committed himself to God.
    When he prayed,
    wings came again;
    still not completely grown,
    they could not carry him this time either.
finally, realizing that impatience
prevented his flying,
he said to himself,
"When wings come the third time,
I'm waiting till they grow strong;
then I can fly successfully."
Thinking in this vein,
wings did indeed grow the third time;
This time he waited for them to fully develop.
    (It seemed to him, he reflected,
    a hundred and fifty years
    between the first and second and third growth of wings.)
Finally, with the third growth of wings,
he applied himself completely,
took off
and landed on a high place with the angel.
    He knocked at the door of the palace
    where the angel had gone.
    The doorkeeper asked,
        "What right have you to come?"
    He answered,
        "I am a Friar Minor."
    The doorkeeper said,
        "Wait and I'll get St. Francis;
        we'll see if he knows you."

While the doorkeeper went in search of the Saint,
the friar looked at the magnificent palace walls;
   They seemed saturated with bright light
   and through them he saw choirs of saints
   and everything taking place inside.
He absorbed himself in looking.
Then St. Francis appeared
with Brothers Bernard and Giles;
   Behind the Saint came
   a whole host of holy men and women,
   followers of Francis on earth,
   so many they seemed uncountable.
Francis said to the doorkeeper,
   "Let him in;
   he's one of my friars."
The moment he got inside,
   he forgot the terrible journey.
The place struck him with such beauty,
   the horrible past seemed
   never to have happened.
Then Francis guided him about,
showing him marvellous things everywhere.
Francis said,
   "My son,
   you have to go back to earth
   for seven days.
   During that period,
   get yourself ready with great care;
   I will come to get you,
   and you will live with me here
   in this home for the blessed."
Francis, clothed in a wondrous coat
   decorated with stars,
   also wore the five wounds of Jesus;
   The wounds shone like stars,
   lighting up the palace
   with the brightest of rays.
      Brother Bernard wore a crown of stars;

Brother Giles stood in radiant light.
Many recognizable saints,
whom the friar never saw on earth,
stood there.
Saying good-bye to Francis,
the friar returned reluctantly to earth.
He awoke from his vision.
As he came to himself,
the friars rang the bell for
the first worship of the day.
His vision had lasted from
worship at the dead of night
to the first worship at dawn.
Seven days after his vision,
the friar fell ill with a fever;
on the eighth day, Francis came as promised
and, with a great many glorious saints,
they directed his spirit to the
Kingdom of Everlasting Life.
Christ's Name be praised. Amen.

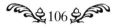

XXVII

Two Distinguished Scholars

St. Francis went to Bologna.
Everyone rushed to see him there;
in fact, he could hardly reach the square
where men, women and scholars had come.
 Francis climbed to a high place
 from which he preached to the people,
 as the Spirit directed him.
  The inspiration of his message
  made the people feel they listened to an angel
  rather than to a mere man.
   His inspired words pierced hearts;
   the arrows hit everyone,
   and many repented,
   converting to Christ.
Two scholars of noble birth
stood in the town's square with the people;
 One named Pellegrino,
 The other called Riccieri.
  Both felt the touch of the Spirit
  as Brother Francis preached.
   They approached Francis:
    "We want to leave the world
    to become your friars."
Well, St. Francis knew the revelation
sent by God to these men:
 He knew they would lead
 holy lives in the Order.
 Sharing in their enthusiasm,
 Francis welcomed them happily:
  "Pellegrino, you will lead

a life of humility;
Riccieri, you will serve
the brothers."
That's exactly what happened:
Brother Pellegrino never got ordained;
he remained a layperson,
even though very learned in Church law.
This humility became the vehicle
for perfecting him.
Brother Bernard, an early disciple of Francis,
said he had rarely seen one so perfect.
Brother Pellegrino went to heaven,
having performed miracles
before his death;
he performed miracles after death, too.
Brother Riccieri served the brothers
with devotion and unfailing consistency.
He lived in unusual holiness and humility,
very close to St. Francis
who revealed many secrets to him.
He became Minister of a province called
the March of Ancona,
and ruled it a long time
in peace and very wisely.
But after some time,
God permitted him to have a big temptation.
It upset him,
causing great distress.
He fasted, wept, prayed
and disciplined himself day and night.
But the temptation stayed;
he suffered depression;
he felt God had abandoned him.
He decided to see St. Francis:
"If Francis treats me graciously,
as he usually does,
I can believe God will help me.
If Francis turns me away,

then I will know God has indeed
abandoned me."
So he went to see Francis,
gravely ill at the time,
in the bishop's palace at Assisi.
God told Francis about the temptation,
and about the friar's depression,
and the reason for the visit.
Brother Francis called Brothers Leo
and Masseo:
"Go quickly to the son I love so much,
Brother Riccieri;
Give him a hug for me."
So they found Brother Riccieri,
hugged him,
welcomed him, and
told him of Francis' special love.
Instantly Riccieri's soul
filled up with love and comfort,
much to his enormous relief!
With great praise to God,
he went to find Francis lying ill.
Even though St. Francis lay terribly ill,
when he heard Brother Riccieri's steps,
he got out of bed, and
even walked to meet him.
He embraced him warmly:
"Brother Riccieri,
my very dear son,
of all the world's friars,
you live specially in my heart."
Francis traced the sign of the cross
on Brother Riccieri's forehead,
then spoke:
"My very dear son,
God allowed you to be tempted
for your own great gain,
but if you want no further gain,

you may have release of spirit."
Almost at once the temptation left,
so completely he seemed never to have
experienced the temptation.
He never suffered depression again.
In praise of Christ. Amen.

XXVIII

Brother Bernard in Ecstasy

God often gives much grace
to the poor who leave the world
to follow Christ.
    God did this for Brother Bernard,
    who was from Quintaville.
After putting on the habit of St. Francis,
many times God wrapped this friar in Himself,
as Bernard meditated on heavenly things.
    For example,
    once while in church for Mass,
    his mind carried him away to God;
        He absorbed himself in God
        so completely
        that he saw nothing when the priest
        consecrated the Blessed Sacrament.
            Bernard did not kneel;
            he did not cover his head
            (as others did);
            But, motionless,
            he looked upwards for hours,
                from worship in the dead of night
                till noon.
He returned to himself after noon prayers,
then walked through the friary
telling everyone in a loud voice:
        "Brothers! Brothers! Brothers!
        Everyone promised a palace with gold
        would do anything to get it,
        even carry a sack of manure,
        to have possession of so beautiful a house."

Well, Brother Bernard lived
constantly in God;
He kept his eye on the heavenly palace
promised to those who love God.
For fifteen years Bernard went about
with his face and heart lifted to heaven.
    All this time he never ate till filled,
    though he took some of the food served at meals,
        because he had to deny himself some pleasure of taste
        to enjoy what food he did eat.
    By this abstinence,
    he got a clear mind,
        an enlightened mind too.
        Very learned clergy
        asked hard questions,
        got obscure Bible passages cleared up,
        solved the greatest of difficulties.
            His mind entirely freed from the world,
            he flew to the heights of meditation
            like a swallow soaring;
            at times he stayed twenty or thirty days
            at the highest elevations,
            lost in heaven's world.
Because of this,
Brother Giles believed no one else
had received such a gift;
    Brother Bernard, said Brother Giles,
    could even "feed as he flew,"
    like the swallow.
Brother Francis
often talked with Brother Bernard freely
day or night,
because of this sublime gift.
Occasionally they lost themselves in contemplation
all night long in the forest
where they had come to talk about Jesus Christ,
the Eternally Blessed One.

XXIX

The Devil and Brother Ruffino

Brother Ruffino,
one of the noblest friars of Assisi,
friend of St. Francis,
person of much sanctity,
    suffered temptation about predestination.
    Result?
    Depression!
Why?
    The devil made him think
    Damnation!
    Damned because not counted among
    the predestined for heaven.
    Therefore, whatever he did for the Order
    came to nothing.
The temptation stayed with Ruffino daily,
but he never had the courage to reveal it to
St. Francis.
    But he never gave up his prayers
    or assigned fasts.
        The enemy fought back with
            multiplied sorrows,
            additional inward conflicts,
            hallucinations, even.
Once the devil came
looking like the Crucified:
    "Brother Ruffino,
    give up penance and prayer;
    you're not one of the elect.
    Let me tell you,
    I know whom I have chosen.

Therefore, ignore the son of Peter Bernardone
if he says you're in the Kingdom.
      Don't quiz him;
      obviously he cannot know
      (nor can anyone else)
      something I, the Son of God, know.
So, know for certain that you're damned.
I haven't elected Peter Bernardone's son either;
Neither you nor he, your father, can come to heaven.
No one who follows Francis can enter."
At this the devil quickly withdrew,
leaving Brother Ruffino plunged into deep depression
because of this Prince of Darkness.
He lost every bit of trust and love for Francis
and could not disclose a thing.
      No matter! Everything Ruffino wouldn't tell,
      the Holy Spirit revealed to Francis;
            So when Francis knew of the friar's
            terrible peril,
            he told Brother Masseo to go to him.
But Ruffino answered Masseo with a grumble:
      "I have nothing to do with Francis."
Masseo spoke divinely,
sensing the devil's deception:
      "Dear Brother Ruffino,
      surely you know Francis is like an angel;
      he has given illumination to many;
      through him God gives many graces.
      Therefore, I want you to come see him
      immediately.
      Clearly, the devil deceived you."
Well, now Ruffino went to St. Francis.
      Watching him coming from a distance,
      Francis called to him:
            "You unhappy fellow;
            Whom did you listen to?"
      When the two came close together,
      Francis told Ruffino, in detail,

all about his temptations,
inward and outward;
>Then he proved with finality
>that the devil had appeared as Christ,
>and therefore Ruffino should ignore
>every suggestion.
"So when the devil says again,
'You're damned,'
answer: 'I will drop dung on your mouth.'
Proof that the devil,
not Christ, spoke,
will be that — upon hearing your reply —
the devil will leave.
This will also teach you that
the devil means to harden your heart
against everything good;
>But Christ never hardens the hearts
>of His faithful ones;
>Rather, He melts hearts,
>as He says by the Prophet Ezekiel:
>>'I will take away their heart of stone,
>>and give them a heart of flesh.'"
Well now, Ruffino saw the accuracy of St. Francis' description,
as he analyzed the whole course of the temptations.
The words touched him.
He wept very much
and requested the Saint's prayers.
More! He confessed his mistake
in hiding the temptation.
>He got full assurance and comfort
>by the help of St. Francis,
>and changed totally.
At last St. Francis said,
"Go to confession;
do not give up your discipline
of regular prayer.
Know this:
>Your temptation will help you greatly,

and comfort you, too.
          You will see this shortly."
So Brother Ruffino returned to his cell in the forest,
and continued praying with lots of tears.
The enemy came back looking like Christ:
          "Brother Ruffino,
          didn't I instruct you not to believe
          the son of Peter Bernardone?
          Don't fatigue yourself with
          tears and prayers;
          No need for that, for you're damned."
Instantly, Brother Ruffino answered:
          "Open your mouth so I can drop dung on it!"
At this, the devil made haste to leave,
and this brought on a great storm
in the mountains and among the rocks,
which began to shatter.
          The pieces of fallen stones
          stayed where they landed a long time.
                    But, before settling,
                    rocks hit one another
                    making sparks,
                    creating an eerie atmosphere
                    throughout the valley.
At this terrible rumbling,
St. Francis and the friars
came out of the friary to see
these astonishing fireworks.
          To this day the vast ruin of stones
          appears scattered here and there.
Now Brother Ruffino knew without a doubt
that the devil had deceived him.
          He went back to Francis,
          threw himself at his feet in
          deep regret,
          confessing his fault.
St. Francis brought him comfort
with tender words,

and put his heart at total peace.
Ruffino returned to his cell
in a prayerful attitude.
Then! Christ Himself appeared to Ruffino,
stirring his soul to great love.
"My son,
you did right trusting Francis.
The devil upset you;
but know that I am your Master,
and to give you fresh assurance,
I grace you with freedom from sadness;
No more depression so long as you live!"
After these words, Christ went away,
but He left Ruffino with enormous joy,
grand purity of soul,
a renewed mind —
all this sent him into ecstasy
for the entire day and night.
From this time onward,
Brother Ruffino knew the
inward confirmation of grace
and the assurance of his salvation.
Now an entirely changed person,
he wanted to pray all day and all night,
all the time
pondering divine revelation.
That's why Brother Francis used to say,
"Jesus canonized Ruffino in *this* life."
So Francis called him *Saint* to everybody
(but not to Ruffino himself)
even though he still lived on earth.

XXX

St. Francis and Brother Ruffino
Preach Naked in Assisi

Constantly meditating,
Brother Ruffino absorbed himself in God,
absent from the world of sense,
silent and seldom talking.
He had no gift for preaching,
no nice flow of public speech.
Nonetheless, St. Francis ordered him
to go to Assisi and preach
as God directed him.
    So Ruffino answered:
        "Respected Father,
        I plead with you to let me off;
        don't make me preach.
        You know very well
        I don't have the grace of preaching;
        I am simple and ignorant."
But Francis said,
    "You have not obeyed me right away,
    therefore, by order of holy obedience
    go to Assisi stripped,
    wearing only your underwear.
        You must go into a church
        and preach stripped."
Hearing this order,
    Brother Ruffino stripped,
    went to Assisi,
    made his way into a church,
    knelt before the altar,

then mounted the pulpit
and began preaching.
When the people saw this,
children and adults alike
laughed and said,
　　"Just look at that!
　　These friars do such foolish penances
　　that their senses leave them;
　　they become unbalanced."
Meanwhile, St. Francis pondered Brother Ruffino's
instant obedience,
his nobility,
the respect he had in Assisi,
and the uncivil character of Francis' command.
　　Well! St. Francis scolded himself:
　　　"You son of Peter Bernardone,
　　　how do you come by such presumption?
　　　Miserable little fellow,
　　　you ordered Ruffino,
　　　one of the noblest persons in Assisi,
　　　to preach stripped,
　　　like a madman before all the people.
　　　By God's help,
　　　you will do exactly what you
　　　dictated that Ruffino do."
Thus motivated,
he stripped and went to Assisi,
taking along Brother Leo
　　　who carried Francis' and Ruffino's habits.
When the Assisi citizens saw Francis,
they mocked him too!
　　They assumed both Ruffino and Francis
　　had gone quite mad from too much penance.
As Francis entered the church,
Ruffino still stood preaching:
　　"Dearest friends,
　　turn your backs on the world,
　　forget sin,

give generously to others,
— if you want to avoid hell.
Put God's commandments into action;
love Him and your neighbors
— if you want to go to heaven.
Practice repentance
— if you want the Kingdom of Heaven."
Then St. Francis, also stripped,
went into the pulpit
and addressed the flock under inspiration
about disdaining the world,
about sacred penance,
about sacrificial living,
about the Kingdom of Heaven,
about the nakedness and humiliation
of our Lord Jesus Christ during His passion.
All those listening in the church,
a great many people,
now started weeping loudly
with very much devotion.
Then this sense of devotion
spread throughout Assisi.
That day Christ's sufferings
got to the heart of the people
more than at any time before.
The people knew themselves built up,
also comforted,
by the sermons of Francis and Ruffino.
Francis now dressed Ruffino and himself.
Clothed again, they went back to
the friary at Portiuncula,
lifting praises to God
who had graced them to
overcome themselves,
die to self,
build up the flock of Jesus by example,
and show the sheep how to turn their backs
on the world.

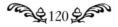
120

The people found themselves all the more devoted
to the two men that day;
Respect for them grew so much
that the people considered themselves blessed
even to touch their clothes.
In praise of Christ the Blessed. Amen.

XXXI

God's Revelation to St. Francis About His Friars

Jesus says in the Gospel record,
    "I know My sheep and they know Me."
Likewise, Francis knew his sheep.
    Francis, the good shepherd,
    knew because God told him
    about the pluses and minuses
    of his friars.
        Accordingly, he knew how to
        bring healing where needed,
        humble the proud ones,
        lift self-esteem in the discouraged.
An example of his divine insight:
    Once in a friary
    discussing God with the friars,
    Brother Ruffino did not appear.
        Ruffino had gone to the forest
        to contemplate God.
Well, when Ruffino finally came out of the woods,
he passed by at a distance from the others,
and St. Francis saw him.
        St. Francis, with Ruffino in the background,
        said to the brothers:
            "Identify the holiest soul
            God possesses on earth."
    They all named St. Francis.
        But Francis declared,
            "Very dear friends,
            I am the most worthless soul
            God possesses on earth.
            But do you see Ruffino

fresh from the woods?
God revealed to me that
his soul is one of the three
most holy souls on earth.
That's why I do not hesitate to
call him *Saint*
even during his lifetime,
for his spirit has found itself
deep in God by grace.
Revered in heaven,
Our Lord has canonized Ruffino."
But St. Francis never called him *Saint*
in Ruffino's presence.
Also by divine revelation,
Francis knew about the faults
of the friars.
He saw right through Brother Elias
and often faced him with his pride.
He also knew ahead of time that
John of Cappella would hang himself
by the neck.
He became aware, too, of the
friar grasped at the throat
by the devil,
when that friar disobeyed.
Many other pluses and minuses Francis knew,
all by divine revelation from the Blessed Christ. Amen.

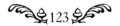

XXXII

Brother Masseo's Deep Desire for Humility

Francis' first companions
worked very hard to
turn their backs on materialism and
turn their faces toward spiritual riches.
    One day while all together,
    the friars talked about God.
        "Once upon a time," began one friar,
        "a man became a great friend of God.
        He possessed grace for
            action,
            contemplation,
            and humility
            (he believed himself the worst of sinners).
            This humility set him apart as special,
            and confirmed him in God's grace;
            it also facilitated more and more growth
                in God's gifts and virtues,
                and never allowed him to fall into sin."
Brother Masseo heard all this and
his heart flamed with desire for humility,
        knowing this would help him find
        the treasures of eternal life.
        So fired was he, in fact, that
        he lifted his face to heaven
        and fervently vowed to take no pleasure
        in the world until humility
        established itself in his soul.
            That's why he now kept himself
            almost entirely confined to his cell,
            fasting,

praying,
weeping, and
    begging God for the humility
    which that friend of God had,
    and without which Masseo felt
    he deserved hell.
Well, totally given to this enterprise
for many days,
Masseo went into the woods one day where he
    wept,
    prayed in grieving tones,
    and cried out for
    God's gift.
    Because God likes to hear the humble,
    a voice out of heaven said,
        "Brother Masseo! Brother Masseo!"
    Brother Masseo sensed that Christ spoke.
        "My Lord, my Lord,"
        he answered.
    Christ replied,
        "What will you give for this grace?"
    Masseo answered:
        "I will give you my eyes."
    Christ responded,
        "I want you to have humility
        and your eyes too."
    With this, Christ said no more.
Masseo now felt full of joy,
for Christ had given him both
    the grace of humility and
    the grace of God's light.
You can see why
he just could not stop being happy.
Now, too, he thought of himself
the least of all persons in the world.
    Often in prayer,
    he sounded like a dove
    cooing softly — "ooh, ooh."

In this mood,
his joy wrote itself on
his face
and revealed itself in
his heart.
Asked by Brother James of Fallerone why
he never altered the tone of his happy praying,
Masseo replied,
"When you've found complete satisfaction,
why change it?"
Give glory to Jesus Christ. Amen.

XXXIII

The Cross on the Loaves

St. Clare was
a devout follower of
   the Crucified Christ,
a beautiful flower of
   St. Francis the leader,
a person of such sanctity that
   bishops,
   cardinals,
   even the Pope
      delighted in seeing her
      and in hearing what she said,
      and came to visit her.
Once the Pope came visiting the convent
to hear her talk about God
and heavenly matters.
As they spoke about spiritual things,
   St. Clare asked to have the tables set,
   and bread put at each place;
   the Pope would bless the loaves.
Their conversation about spiritual affairs ended;
St. Clare knelt with appropriate reverence,
then asked him to bless the table loaves.
   The Holy Father replied,
      "My faithful sister, Clare,
      I want you yourself to bless the bread,
      tracing the sign of the cross over it,
      for you have given yourself to that cross
      completely."
   Clare responded like this:
      "My Holy Father,

please do excuse me from this assignment,
for I only deserve rebuke;
I do not feel worthy to give the blessing
while you stand here."
Then the Pope said,
"I don't want you to feel presumptuous,
so act in holy obedience
by tracing the sign of the cross
and blessing the loaves."
Clare, true daughter of obedience,
blessed the loaves with great devotion
and used the sign of the cross.
Then the marvel!
The sign of the cross
appeared at once on each loaf.
Some loaves the people ate;
others they set aside
to preserve the miracle.
The Pope ate some bread
after he saw the miracle,
then blessed Clare and went away.
Sister Ortolana,
mother of Clare,
lived at the convent too;
so did Clare's sister, Agnes.
All three experienced fresh blessing,
the filling of the Holy Spirit,
as did many other nuns.
No wonder St. Francis sent lots of sick folks
to the nuns;
they sent up healing prayers
by the sign of the cross,
and many experienced actual healing.
We praise Christ. Amen.

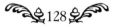

XXXIV

The King of France Visits Brother Giles
Without a Word

St. Louis, King of France,
made a pilgrimage to see holy places
all over the world.
 He heard about Brother Giles' holiness;
 Brother Giles was one of Francis' first companions.
Louis determined to see this Brother Giles.
 That's why the King went to Perugia,
 where Brother Giles lived.
  King Louis knocked on the friary door,
  dressed as a poor and common pilgrim.
  He had with him only a few friends.
   With single-minded perseverance,
   he insisted on seeing Brother Giles,
   but the King never identified himself.
The doorkeeper told Brother Giles
a pilgrim had come to see him,
that he waited at the door.
 Well! God told Giles the man waiting
 was none other than the King of France.
  That's why Giles ran from his cell
  with such enthusiasm.
   They had never seen one another,
   yet both knelt devoutly,
   no questions asked;
   embraced
   and kissed tenderly
   as if long-standing friends.
    They said not a single word,
    but stood in silence
    embracing one another,

the outward symbol of their affection.
   After quite some time,
   still no words uttered,
   Louis left to continue his pilgrimage
   and Giles returned to his cell.
When King Louis left,
one of the friars asked,
  "Who was that?
  They must have been long-time friends
  to embrace so long."
  One replied that it was Louis, King of France.
  The other friars
  expressed their unhappiness
  that Giles would not say a word.
   "Giles, why did you show so little courtesy
   to the holy King of France;
   he came a long way to see you!
   He wanted your counsel."
    "Very dear brothers," said Giles,·
    "don't be surprised;
    Neither of us could say a word,
    because, as soon as we embraced,
    Wisdom's divine light
    opened his heart to me
    and *vice versa*.
    Communication took place far better
    than if we had talked.
    Greater consolation, too.
     You see,
     if we had used words,
     what we sensed inside
     could have come only to
     frustrated expression.
     God's hidden mysteries don't yield
     to human language very well.
    You must know that the King
    went away wonderfully strengthened."
In praise of Christ. Amen.

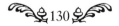

XXXV

St. Clare Is Miraculously Transported

Seriously ill one Christmas Eve,
St. Clare could not worship in the church
with the other nuns.
    While others went,
    she stayed in bed.
    She grieved about this.
But her Spouse, Jesus Christ,
unwilling to leave her without comfort,
transported her by angels to St. Francis' church.
    She stayed for worship and
    Midnight Mass.
        She also received Holy Communion,
        then Christ transported her home again.
When the nuns returned from worship
in San Damiano,
they said to her,
        "Dear mother, Sister Clare,
        we received such comfort on
        this holy Nativity night!
        We wish only that God would have
        permitted you to go."
St. Clare replied like this:
        "I praise and thank my Lord
        Jesus Christ, the Blessed One.
        My sisters and very dear daughters,
        I did indeed attend worship
        on this most holy night,
        and to my great comfort.
        St. Francis interceded for me,
        and, by God's grace, I worshipped

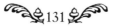

in the church of our Father, St. Francis.
I heard every song,
I listened to the organ,
I witnessed everything with my eyes
and my spiritual senses, too.
Naturally, for this very great favor,
I praise and give thanks to our Lord,
Jesus Christ."
In praise of Christ. Amen.

XXXVI

St. Francis Explains Brother Leo's Vision

Brother Leo cared for St. Francis
when he suffered
from a terrible illness.
    Praying beside Francis,
    Leo saw himself transported in spirit
    by an enormous and rushing river.
        In his vision,
        he saw friars weighed down
        as they started to cross the river.
            Thrust into rushing waters,
            the brothers drowned.
        Some brothers got a third of the way across,
        others half way;
        some almost across.
            But all fell,
            due to the turbulence
            and the weighty things they carried.
                Seeing all this,
                Brother Leo's heart went out
                to all the brothers.
        All at once,
        Leo saw another great group
        of friars;
        These had no burdens,
        but their faces shone with the glory
        of holy poverty.
            These stepped into the river
            and crossed with no difficulty.
    After this vision,
    Leo came back to himself.

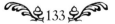
133

St. Francis knew in his spirit that
Brother Leo had had a vision.
    He asked Leo to reveal the vision;
    Leo told him every detail.
Francis had this to say:
    "You saw the truth.
    The big river stands for
    the world.
    The brothers who drowned
    refused to follow the Gospel;
    especially they refused to give up
    everything they owned.
    Those who crossed with no problem
    didn't search for,
    nor did they possess,
    any worldly thing.
        Their humble clothes
            and plain food
                show their contentment
                just following the naked Christ
                of the cross.
    They enjoy carrying
    the gentle burdens of His cross
    and the yoke of holy obedience.
        That explains their passage from earth to heaven
        with no difficulty."
We praise Christ. Amen.

XXXVII

The Conversion of a Nobleman Who Became a Friar

Late one evening,
Francis, the servant of Christ,
called on a prestigious nobleman.
    Francis and his companion
    found a courteous reception;
    In fact, they were treated
    like angels.
Well! Francis could not help but
respond to the nobleman with a lot of love.
    After all,
    Francis and friend arrived at a bad hour,
    yet the nobleman gave them a hug,
            gave them a kiss,
            washed their feet,
            dried their feet,
            made a big fire,
            set a well-supplied table.
As they sat eating,
the nobleman went right on
serving them with enthusiasm.
    Finished eating,
    Francis and his friend listened
    to what the nobleman said:
        "Father, I give you myself
        and all I own;
        If you ever need clothing,
        or anything else,
        buy it and I will pay the bill.
        By God's grace,

I can do that.
Because God gives me so many things,
I, in turn, want to give them to the poor."
This great courtesy,
couched in the most generous language,
aroused such love in Francis that
he said to his companion as they left:
"Without a doubt,
this generous and grateful man,
so loving and courteous,
would bring a whole new dimension of good
to our friary.
You know, of course, that
courtesy is a godly virtue.
After all,
God Himself, out of courtesy,
gives the sun and rain,
even to bad as well as good people.
Courtesy is the sister of charity
which puts out the fire of hatred
and fans the flame of love.
I see divine courtesy in
this good nobleman;
That's why I would love having him
a member of our group.
So let's go back to him some day
to find out if God has called him
to join us in His service.
In the meantime,
let's ask God to nudge him and
give him grace to act on the nudge."
A marvelous thing followed
after St. Francis' prayer:
God put this very desire into
the nobleman's heart.
A few days later
St. Francis said to his companion,
"Brother, let's go to that

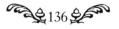

courteous nobleman;
I feel like trusting God
to call this courteous man
to give himself to us all
as a companion."
They went.
Approaching the house,
Francis said,
    "Wait here for awhile
    because I want to pray first,
    asking God for success,
    so that everything will please Christ,
        the One of Compassion,
        that even we the weak ones,
        can take the nobleman out of the world."
Saying that,
Francis started praying
in a place where the nobleman could see him.
    As the nobleman watched Francis praying,
    he saw Francis standing before Christ,
    who was shining in a very bright light;
    he saw Francis raised up,
    even suspended in air for a time.
        God showed this to the nobleman
        to call him from the world.
    He left the palace,
    actually running to St. Francis.
    The nobleman knelt
    and asked that Francis
    pray with him.
Now St. Francis knew God had answered
his prayer;
he got up and embraced the nobleman
with great joy and enthusiasm,
kissed him,
and devoutly thanked God
who had given such a knight
to the friary.

The nobleman asked Francis,
    "What do you want me to do?
    I'm prepared to give what I have
    to the poor,
    and to follow Christ with you,
    unhampered by material things."
So Francis told him
to distribute all his possessions to the poor,
enter the Order,
live in repentance,
and lead a holy life.
In praise of Christ. Amen.

XXXVIII

St. Francis Prays for Brother Elias

Saint Francis and Brother Elias
once lived in the same friary.
    At that time the Lord
    revealed to Francis that
    Brother Elias would lose his soul
    and leave the Order.
        Following this revelation,
        Brother Elias rejected Francis;
        so much so that Francis could not
        talk to him,
        even avoided Elias when he saw him coming.
Brother Elias began to get the message:
    I displease Francis.
    He wanted to ask why.
        He walked toward Francis one day;
        Francis tried to avoid him,
        but Elias courteously held him,
        then asked why Francis did not want
        to associate with him.
Francis answered:
    "God told me that your sins
    will take you out of our Order and
    keep you from heaven."
Elias then said,
    "I plead with you, reverend father,
    by Christ's love
    not to cast me away,
    but to help like a good shepherd,
    thus imitating Christ,
    by finding and rescuing the lost sheep

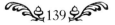

139

which will perish without you.
Please talk to God for me.
Your prayers may please Him
so He will rescue me,
for Scripture shows God can change
a sentence if the sinner changes.
I have great faith in your prayers;
so much so that if I lived in hell
and you interceded,
I would find some relief.
You see, then, why I plead with you
to ask God,
Who came to save sinners,
to have mercy on me, a sinner."
Brother Elias said all this with
deep feeling and lots of tears.
St. Francis,
with the mercy of a father,
promised to pray and did so.
God revealed to Francis that
He heard the prayer,
that He had cancelled the sentence,
that Elias would go to heaven.
Nonetheless, he would leave the Order
and die outside it.
And that is what happened.
When King Frederick of Sicily
turned rebel against the Church,
he and his rebel companions
suffered excommunication by the Pope.
Now, the King and others considered Brother Elias
one of the wisest men in the world.
Would you believe Brother Elias
stood by King Frederick and the rebels?
That Brother Elias rebelled against the Church
and left the Order?
The Pope excommunicated Elias
and took away his Franciscan habit.

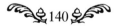

While excommunicated,
Elias became terribly ill.
    Elias' brother,
    also a member of the Order,
    heard about Elias' illness.
    This good friar went to see Elias:
        "Very dear brother,
        I am horribly sad that you
            left the Church,
            left the Order,
            and will die like this.
        But if you know some way that I
        can rescue you,
        I will joyfully help you."
Brother Elias replied,
    "I see only one way to help me:
        Go to the Pope,
        beg him by Christ's love
            and for Francis' sake
            (for whose teaching I left the world),
        to cancel my excommunication and
        to return my habit of the Order."
The brother promised to do that —
        gladly, in fact,
        for his brother's salvation.
He left on foot to see the Holy Father,
pleading with all humility
to help Brother Elias,
out of love for Christ and St. Francis.
    This pleased God,
    for the Pope said to
    return to Brother Elias,
    and — if still alive — to
    tell him the Pope cancelled the sentence.
    He could tell Elias, too,
    to wear the habit of St. Francis.
The brother left happily,
and hurried to Brother Elias.

He found him close to death,
so he gave Elias the Pope's message.
He put the habit on Elias again,
and Brother Elias died.
Brother Elias' request had not been in vain;
St. Francis' prayers saved him.
Praises be to Christ. Amen.

XXXIX

St. Anthony of Padua Preaches Under Inspiration

St. Anthony of Padua,
a companion of St. Francis,
was a divinely chosen vehicle of
the Spirit.
    St. Francis used to call St. Anthony
    his bishop.
Once he preached at a conference
attended by the Pope and cardinals,
and men from many nations: Greeks,
                        Latins,
                        Frenchmen,
                        Germans,
                        Slavs,
                        English,
                        and others.
In the power of the Spirit,
Anthony preached effectively,
                devoutly,
                graciously,
                powerfully;
And everybody from all these nations,
heard and understood him.
    They all listened in shock,
    reminded of the first Pentecost,
    when the Holy Spirit spoke to all,
    no matter what their language.
Everyone said of St. Anthony,
    "He comes from Spain,
    but all of us understand him!"
The Pope said,

"We can call this man
the Ark of the Covenant and
a treasure of Scripture truth."
We praise Christ. Amen.

XL

St. Anthony Preaches to the Fishes

The Lord made clear,
on one occasion,
the unusual sanctity of His
very faithful servant, St. Anthony.
    Christ rebuked the foolishness of heretics
    by using fish,
just as He cried out against Balaam,
in the Old Testament, through a donkey.
    Studying in Rimini,
    where many heretics lived,
    Anthony attempted to lead them
    back to true light and true faith.
        He preached to them many days,
        talking about faith in Christ
        and belief in the Holy Scriptures.
    The heretics would not listen,
    having hardened their hearts to
    become obstinate sinners.
One day Anthony went to where the river and the sea
come together;
There he preached to the fish:
    "Hear God's Word,
    fish of the water;
    for the infidels will not hear."
After these words of invitation,
an enormous shoal of fish came near the shore.
    Large fish, small and middle-sized ones;
    no one had seen so many.
    They lifted their heads out of the water,
    looked at Anthony and listened

with perfect peace, gentleness and order.
The smaller fish stayed closest to shore,
and the medium-sized next,
and the largest in the deepest water.
Arranged in this order,
St. Anthony preached like this
to the fish:
"My brothers and sisters of the fish world,
You find praising your Creator
a very natural exercise,
for He gives you a perfect living environment:
You can swim in sweet or salt water,
you have many places to hide in a storm,
you have plenty of food.
When your Creator made you,
He ordered you to multiply,
and He put His blessing on you.
Later, at the time of the great flood,
God did not let you die like other animals.
He also gave you fins
so you could go where you wish.
Moreover, a fish saved Jonah;
after three days the fish
coughed him up on shore, safely.
Also a fish provided a coin for
Christ when He was poor and
had no money to pay the tax.
Later still, you provided food for
Jesus, the eternal King,
before and after His resurrection.
No wonder you ought to praise God!
He has housed and blessed you many times."
While Anthony talked like this,
the fish opened their mouths,
then lowered their heads,
showing signs of reverence
while praising God as they could.
When Anthony saw this reverence

for God the Creator,
he cried out with great joy:
"Let's thank the eternal God
because the fish honor Him
more than the heretics;
animals with no reasoning power
comprehend His word
better than unbelievers!"
The more Anthony preached,
the more the fish grew in numbers,
and not a single fish left.
The city people,
including the heretics,
heard about the fish,
then went to see the miracle for themselves.
The miracle made them feel remorse,
and the people threw themselves at Anthony's feet
so they could hear the sermon too.
Now Anthony preached with such power
that all the heretics came to Christ.
Anthony made the Catholic faith come alive!
All the faithful Christians
renewed themselves in joy,
and found strength and comfort.
After a while,
St. Anthony blessed the fish
and dismissed them.
Their animated swimming even demonstrated joy.
The people felt happy, too.
St. Anthony stayed at Rimini
for a long time,
preaching and bringing souls to Christ.
Praise to Christ's name. Amen.

XLI

Brother Simon and the Severely Tempted Friar

Towards the beginning of the Order
— when Francis was still alive —
a young fellow from Assisi,
Brother Simon by name,
joined the friars.
>God gave him special gifts:
>>Contemplation,
>>A devoutly elevated mind,
>>Unusual holiness
>>>(he seemed a mirror of sanctity)
>>>— all this confirmed by those
>>>>who know him a long time.

He rarely left his cell
and, when he did, he talked about God.
He had no formal schooling,
yet when he talked about God
>he spoke in great depth and
>revealed the love of Christ;
>>— his words
>>>struck others as supernatural.

Once he stayed in the forest
with Brother James of Massa
the whole night.
>They talked about God
>and about God's love,
>and by morning (according to James)
>the two men wondered where the time had gone.

When Brother Simon sensed
a divine visitation coming,
he experienced delicious peace and

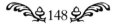

joy in the Spirit.
He would lie on his bed
in perfect serenity,
for the Spirit brought tranquil joy
and peace to his soul,
and also calmness to his body.
In those visitations,
God often elevated Simon's spirit
so that he became insensible
to everything around him.
Once, while lost in God and
dead to the world,
he flamed inside with love,
totally unaware of his body.
A friar, wanting to test the depth
of Simon's unconsciousness,
put a live coal on his bare foot.
Brother Simon felt nothing,
nor did the coal leave a mark,
even though it stayed there so long
that it burned itself out.
At meals,
Brother Simon ate food for his body
but also took food for his soul,
the latter by talking of God.
Simon's holy conversation God used once
to convert a worldly young man;
Vain enough,
he came from nobility
and lived in luxury.
The youth, after conversion,
joined the Order.
Brother Simon received the fellow,
took his secular clothes,
gave him the habit, and
sat with him to instruct him in the Rule.
Well! the devil likes to ruin
all good intentions,

and the new friar soon found himself
plagued by terrible temptations,
especially those of the flesh.
    The poor fellow became completely helpless.
    So he went to Brother Simon:
        "Give me back my clothes;
        I can resist these physical temptations
        no longer."
Brother Simon,
in a great outpouring of love,
asked the young man
to sit with him a while.
    Simon talked of God with such power
    the temptation left.
Later, the temptation returned;
the fellow insisted on his clothes again;
    Once more Brother Simon drove away the
    temptation by talking of God.
This happened several times;
then the temptation came
more forcefully than ever.
    The poor fellow stood utterly paralyzed.
    He went to Simon for his clothes;
    he simply could not stay.
Brother Simon had him sit beside him
as before;
He talked to him about God;
the youth leaned on Simon
in terrible sadness and despair.
    Brother Simon's pity made him
    lift his eyes to heaven
    to pray very intensely.
        Well! That young man became ecstatic
        when Brother Simon's prayer was granted
        by God.
            Presently the youthful friar
            returned to himself,
            all temptation gone —

just as if it had never come!
>The fire of temptation was translated
>into the fire of God's Spirit
>by contact with that glowing coal,
>Brother Simon.
>So the young man burned with God's love
>and love for others.
>>His transformation proved so great
>>that when a bad person got arrested
>>and authorities said his eyes
>>had to be put out,
>>the compassionate friar went to
>>the Governor and the full Council,
>>wept and pleaded,
>>asking that only one eye be put out,
>>and that the friar give one of his own eyes
>>so the criminal would not go totally blind.
>>>The Governor and Council
>>>touched by this fervor and love,
>>>gave the criminal a full pardon.

One day Brother Simon,
praying in the forest
and feeling deep peace of soul,
heard some rooks caw so loudly they
disturbed him.
>He asked them,
>in Jesus' name,
>to fly away and stay away.
>>The birds went,
>>never to return,
>>not even to the neighboring districts.
>>>Everyone in the province of Fermo
>>>(where the friary was located)
>>>heard about this miracle.
In praise of the name of Jesus Christ. Amen.

Further Reading and Viewing

Armstrong, Regis J. and Ignatius C. Brady, Translators and
Introduction (and Preface by John Vaughn), *Francis
and Clare: The Complete Works* (New York: Paulist,
1982; The Classics of Western Spirituality series).

Armstrong, Regis J. and Ignatius C. Brady, Translators, *Praying
with Saint Francis* (London: SPCK, 1987).

Blaiklock, E.M. and A.C. Keys, Translators, *The Little Flowers of
St. Francis* (London: Hodder and Stoughton, 1985).

Brother Sun, Sister Moon. Euro International, 1972 (motion
picture).

Brown, Raphael, Translator, *The Little Flowers of St. Francis* (New
York: Image Books, 1958).

Chesterton, G.K., *St. Francis of Assisi* (London: Hodder and
Stoughton, 1923).

Hughes, Serge, Translator, *The Little Flowers of Saint Francis and
Other Franciscan Writings* (New York: New American
Library, 1964).

Kossak, Zofia, *Blessed Are the Meek* (Rulka Langer, Translator;
New York: Roy Publishers, 1944).

Sherley-Price, Leo, Translator, *The Little Flowers of Saint Francis
with Five Considerations on the Sacred Stigmata* (Balti-
more, MD: Penguin Books, 1959).

Williamson, Glen, *Repair My House* (Carol Stream, IL: Creation
House, 1973).

ST PAULS

This book was designed and published by St. Pauls/Alba House, the publishing arm of the Society of St. Paul, an international religious congregation of priests and brothers dedicated to serving the Church through the communications media. For information regarding this and associated ministries of the Pauline Family of Congregations, write to the Vocation Director, Society of St. Paul, 7050 Pinehurst, Dearborn, Michigan 48126. Phone (313) 582-3798 or check our internet site, www.albahouse.org